Written by
Michelle Powers, Teri Barenborg,
Tari Sexton, and Lauren Monroe

Editors: Christie Weltz and Jasmine Tabrizi
Designer/Production: Kammy Peyton
Art Director: Moonhee Pak
Project Director: Stacey Faulkner

© 2017 Creative Teaching Press Inc., Cypress, CA 90630
Reproduction of activities in any manner for use in the classroom and not for commercial sale is permissible.
Reproduction of these materials in any manner, in whole or in part, for an entire school or for a school system is strictly prohibited.

DEDICATION

This book is dedicated to all of the educators and children who have inspired us to make education a hands-on experience and, most importantly, instilled within us a lifelong love of learning.

ACKNOWLEDGMENTS

First and foremost, we would like to thank our families and friends who have supported us in so many ways—from the steadfast support of our chosen career path and passion all the way through the inspiration and creation of this series of books. Each of us has an amazing support system that has not only encouraged us but also made it possible for us to devote our time to this project. A sincere thank-you to our colleagues, both past and present, as well as all the educators who have inspired us to create a collection of lessons that encourage students to grow and take ownership of their learning. Without the continued support and encouragement of our dear friend Lynn Howard, these books would not have been possible.

Our school district, St. Lucie Public Schools, known for being the first Kids at Hope school district in the state of Florida, motivated us to build a culture of learning where students state daily that "All children are capable of success. No exceptions." This mindset, along with the work of Carol Dweck and her focus on self-efficacy through a growth mindset, has inspired us to develop lessons that encourage problem solving and perseverance, allowing students to learn from their mistakes.

We would like to thank the various teachers who have opened their doors to us and, more importantly, the students in those classrooms who have tested these exciting lessons during their development. These teachers have allowed us to model, motivate, and encourage them to transition from the "Sage on the Stage" to a "Guide on the Side," giving students the opportunity to drive their own learning.

FOREWORD

Science instruction has changed. Many of us can remember the traditional lecture and note giving model of instruction that had been used for years. I was very alone in my middle school earth science classroom and had no support, no textbook or curriculum guide. Living day to day with content that was totally unfamiliar to me, I taught the same way to all students and didn't realize that many of them were not engaged or learning. I had to change and allow for more engagement, exploration, and experimentation. It quickly became the way I taught, and students benefited from the problem solving, collaboration, and inquiry-based activities. When I began my science teaching career years ago, I would have appreciated a resource that provided me with a set of classroom lessons that would challenge and motivate my students.

The Next Generation Science Standards are placing a great emphasis on how we "do science" in the classroom. The integration of science, technology, engineering, arts, and math (STEAM) provides multiple opportunities to include problem solving, engineering practices, and literacy while engaging and motivating students in real-world science experiences.

I really like this book. These lessons are perfect for any teacher who may or may not feel comfortable with teaching science. I really like that the lessons are aligned with the 5E Instructional Model (engage, explore, explain, elaborate, and evaluate). Teachers who use the lessons will address the 5E model and challenge their students with the engineering process. The authors are a team of educators who understand how to teach science. Their teaching has evolved from a traditional approach to becoming facilitators of science knowledge. Teri, Lauren, Michelle, and Tari have spent time learning about the changes in science education and how to design effective science classroom environments. As a professional development associate, I spent three years with them as they explored how to create a balanced science program focused on the Next Generation Science Standards. They invested a large amount of time researching what works and implementing those best practices in their classrooms. I have had the opportunity to be in all of their classrooms and see the engagement and excitement as students collaborate on real-world engineering design problems. The teachers continually reinforce the idea that their students ARE scientists and must practice the habits of scientists. A by-product of these teachers' efforts is a book that other teachers can use today in their classrooms to make it exciting to teach and learn about science!

I am honored that Teri, Lauren, Michelle, and Tari asked me to write the foreword for their book. These teachers truly live and breathe quality science teaching and learning. Their passion, dedication, and commitment to effective science instruction make the activities and ideas in this book invaluable to anyone who wants to get excited about STEAM in their classroom.

Lynn F. Howard
Author and Professional Development Associate
Five Easy Steps to a Balanced Science Program

TABLE OF CONTENTS

GETTING STARTED

Introduction 5
How to Use This Book 6
The Standards 13
Integration in the Engineering
Design Challenge 14
STEAM Design Process 15
Recording Information
in a Science Notebook 16

EARTH AND SPACE SCIENCE

Block That Blizzard 20
I Can See Clearly Now 26
Please Rain on My Parade 32
Stellar Sundials 38

ENGINEERING DESIGN

Build a Better Bridge 44
Honk for Hybrids 50
Orca Overcast 56
Stow for the Crow 62

LIFE SCIENCE

Critter Creations 68
Help! I'm Hungry! 74
Invasive Invaders 80
Pesky Pythons 86

PHYSICAL SCIENCE

Blast Off! 92
Eggstra Safe Cars 98
Greenhouse Gadgets 104
Make It Stick 110
On Target 116
Wacky Waterslides 122

APPENDIX

Lesson Plan–Specific Reproducibles 129
Individual Blueprint Design Sheet 136
Group Blueprint Design Sheet 137
Graph 138
Budget Planning Chart 139
STEAM Job Cards 140
Science Notebook Cover 141
STEAM Money 142
STEAM Rubric 144
Glossary 146
Bibliography 151

INTRODUCTION

Science, technology, engineering, art, and math work together to make learning fun!

The Next Generation Science Standards place a greater emphasis on science, technology, engineering, arts, and math (STEAM) in today's classrooms. Schools are implementing and encouraging strong STEAM programs in classrooms in order to provide critical thinking lessons that meet the content standards. STEAM lessons should include problem-solving skills, enhance learning across various disciplines, promote student inquiry, and engage students with real-world situations. Students should be exposed to careers in the STEAM fields and develop skills such as communication, data analysis, following a process, designing a product, and argumentation based on evidence, all while cementing effective collaboration techniques that are necessary for a successful career in STEAM fields.

The lessons in this book are intended to support teachers in implementing the engineering design process in their classroom while integrating national standards from other disciplines. In the engineering design process, teachers become a facilitator rather than the instructional focus. Teachers encourage and guide students to work as a team to find a creative solution without providing step-by-step instructions. The engineering design process shifts away from the long-standing process of the scientific method by placing more emphasis on inquiry. Students are inspired to act as scientists and engineers through the use of sketches, diagrams, mathematical relationships, and literacy connections. By creating their very own models and products based on background information from their studies, students are immediately engaged through a meaningful, rewarding lesson.

Each lesson begins by presenting students with a design challenge scenario, or hook, in order to immediately excite students with a real-world situation that they are on a mission to solve. Students are then given a dilemma, mission, and blueprint design sheet and are asked to collaborate with team members to create several prototypes. Teams are required to choose one prototype to present to their teacher before gathering materials and constructing the chosen design. After testing out their design, teams take part in a class discussion and modify their ideas for redesign and improvement of their prototype. Finally, teams are asked to create a justification piece in order to sell their new prototype. Suggestions for justification projects are provided for each design challenge and include writing a persuasive letter, creating an advertisement or presentation, recording a video, or any other creative ideas they come up with in response to the challenge.

The engaging STEAM design challenge lessons in this book

- Promote analytical and reflective thinking
- Enhance learning across various disciplines
- Encourage students to collaborate to solve real-world design challenges
- Integrate national standards
- Are classroom tested

HOW TO USE THIS BOOK

STEAM design challenges follow the engineering practices that have become recently known in the education field. Engineering practices teach students to solve a problem by designing, creating, and justifying their design. With this model in mind, teachers shift from a "giver of information" to a "facilitator of knowledge." Instead of leading children to the right conclusion through experimental steps, the teacher allows them to work through the process themselves, often changing their plan to improve their original design.

STEAM design challenges allow art to support and enhance the learning of science and math while the engineering process is followed. Students will often use, or be encouraged to use, technology to facilitate their learning. The teacher's role as facilitator allows him or her to guide student thinking by asking questions instead of giving answers. Each lesson covers cross-curricular standards and supports teacher planning for collaboration with other teachers.

Typically, science is not taught as often in elementary school as English, reading, writing, and math, so assignments have been included within the lessons that will assist in giving students skills and practice in those other key subjects.

Lessons focus on key national science standards that are required for many standardized tests and include core English language arts and math standards. National engineering standards as well as national arts and national technology standards are also included in the lessons.

The 5E Instructional Model emphasizes building new ideas using existing knowledge. The components of this model—*Engage, Explore, Explain, Elaborate,* and *Evaluate*—are also a key design feature in the structure of each design challenge. Each design challenge requires the students to respond using mathematical, written, oral, and theatrical skills that are developmentally appropriate while working through each phase of the 5E model.

PHASES OF THE 5E MODEL

ENGAGE
Students make connections between past and present learning and focus their thinking on learning outcomes in the activity.

EXPLORE
Students continue to build on their knowledge of their learning through exploration and manipulation of materials.

EXPLAIN
Students support their understanding of the concepts through verbal or written communication. This is also a time when students may demonstrate new skills and when teachers can introduce new vocabulary.

ELABORATE
Students extend their understanding of concepts by obtaining more information about a topic through new experiences.

EVALUATE
Students assess their understanding of key concepts and skills.

LESSON PLAN FORMAT

Each lesson centers around the Design Challenge Purpose and has two distinct sections—Setting the Stage and STEAM in Action.

- **Setting the Stage** provides an overview of the lesson, suggested time frame, the background knowledge needed for the teacher and students as well as the standards, target vocabulary, and materials needed.

- **STEAM in Action** outlines the step-by-step procedure for implementing the lesson.

LESSON PLAN COMPONENTS

SETTING THE STAGE

Header: This section includes the title, suggested time frame for completing the lesson, and the STEAM acronym, in which the capital letters denote the main disciplines that are highlighted in each particular lesson.

Time: A suggested approximate total time for completing each lesson is provided. Because the amount of time teachers have to teach science varies within different states, districts, schools, and even grade levels, you may need to break up the lesson into smaller segments over the course of several days. Natural breaks occur between design and construction, between construction and testing, and between testing and justification.

You may choose to use the lesson ideas in the Student Development section to deepen prior knowledge or you may have your students use the literacy connections and any reputable websites you are familiar with. The lesson ideas in the Justification section are included as an optional extension of the core lesson. None of the activities before or after the core lesson are included in the time estimates. Refer to the suggested lesson timeline on page 11.

Design Challenge Purpose: This is the statement that sets the stage for the design challenge and outlines student objectives and expectations for what they should learn by completing the design challenge.

Teacher Development: This section provides background information about the science content being addressed in the lesson. Information included assists the teacher in understanding key science concepts. We understand that professional development at the elementary teacher level is often geared toward instructional delivery instead of content, especially in the content area of science. This section is provided to help support teachers who may not be as familiar with science content.

Student Development: This section contains a description of the concepts students will need to understand to complete the design challenge successfully. A link to the STEAM Dreamers website, which has active web links and additional suggested lesson ideas for deepening students' understanding of relevant science concepts, can be found on the inside front cover of this book.

Standards: This section lists specific standards for science, technology, engineering, art, math, and English language arts, along with the science and engineering practices and crosscutting concepts. These standards may apply to the activities in the challenges or in the justifications that follow. Please make sure that you review the standards for each of the lessons. The website for each set of standards is listed on page 13.

Target Vocabulary: This section lists target vocabulary to support and enhance the lesson content and to deepen students' understanding of the terms. These vocabulary terms are related to the academic content that the design challenge focuses on; can be used throughout the design challenge when in group discussion; and are an integral component of the standards covered in the challenge. Reviewing the target vocabulary prior to beginning the design challenge is recommended as students need to apply their knowledge of the science concepts and target vocabulary when solving the challenges. Ultimately, the target vocabulary should be revisited multiple times throughout the lesson.

Materials: This section lists materials and equipment that have been selected for the lessons. All materials are meant to be easy to find, inexpensive to purchase, recycled, or commonly available for free. Substitute with similar items if you have them on hand, or visit www.SteamDreamers.com for substitute suggestions.

Literacy Connections: This section lists books or articles that are meant to be used with students prior to the design challenge in order to strengthen their background knowledge and to enhance the integration of literacy in STEAM. These connections can be used during the daily classroom reading block, during small and/or whole-group instruction.

Current literacy connections for each lesson can be accessed through our website: www.SteamDreamers.com.

STEAM IN ACTION

The Dilemma: This section includes a unique real-world dilemma or scenario that hooks the students and gets them excited to solve the problem. The dilemma may include a plausible circumstance or a wild story designed to make them think. When planning the design of their prototype, student should ask themselves questions such as *Who is the client? What do we need to create? What is the purpose of the creation? What is the ultimate goal?* Students should discuss these questions with other members of their team and record their responses in their science notebooks.

Note: This is the Engage portion of the lesson, as outlined in the 5E Instructional Model.

The Mission: This section includes the defined challenge statement. This is ultimately the goal that the students are trying to reach.

Blueprint Design: This section instructs students on how to focus their thinking in order to solve the problem. Individual team members design their own plans for prototypes and list the pros and cons of their designs. Each team member reviews the Blueprint Design Sheet of every other team member and records the pros and cons he or she sees. The team then chooses which member's design it will move forward with. This is where students have the opportunity to discuss and make decisions based on their analysis on the Individual Blueprint Design Sheets. Students are allowed and encouraged to add their artistic touches to their thinking. Individual and Group Blueprint Design Sheets are found in the Appendix.

Note: This is the Explore portion of the lesson, as outlined in the 5E Instructional Model.

Engineering Design Process: In this section of the lesson, teams will take their group's selected prototype through the engineering design process to create, test, analyze, and redesign as necessary until they have successfully completed their mission.

- The first step in the process is the Engineering Task in which teams will engineer their prototype.

- Students will then test their prototype based upon the mission statement.

- The analysis of their testing will include data collection and determination of success.

- The Redesign and Retest cycle will continue until the team has successfully completed the mission.

Helpful Tips: In this section you'll find suggestions designed to address common issues that may arise during the design challenges. Some tips are geared toward the steps in the engineering design process, and some are more lesson-specific.

Reflections: This section provides suggestions for reflective questions to ask students to help guide and facilitate their thinking at various stages within the engineering design process. It is recommended that students record these questions and their reflections in a science notebook. See pages 16–19 for more information on using a science notebook.

Note: This is the Explain and Elaborate portion of the lesson, as outlined in the 5E Instructional Model.

Justification: This is the stage of the lesson where students apply what they learned in a meaningful and creative way through different mediums, such as technology and the arts. These justifications can occur in many forms: a formal letter, an advertisement, a poem, a jingle, a skit, or a technology-enhanced presentation.

Note: This is the Evaluate portion of the lesson, as outlined in the 5E Instructional Model.

SUGGESTED LESSON TIMELINE

Lesson Progression:

1. Teacher Development/Student Development/Literacy Connections

2. Dilemma/Mission/Blueprint Design

3. Engineering Task/Test Trial/Analyze/Redesign/Reflection

4. Justification

If the lesson will be spread out over multiple days:

Day 1: Teacher Development/Student Development/Literacy Connections

Day 2: Dilemma/Mission/Blueprint Design

Day 3: Engineering Task/Test Trial

Days 4-6: Analyze/Redesign/Reflection (Can be spread over 3 days)

Days 7-8: Justification

THE APPENDIX

Lesson-Specific Activity Pages: Some lessons include specific activity pages for enhancing or completing the design challenges. They are found in the Appendix section.

Blueprint Design Sheets: Every lesson requires students to first use the Individual Blueprint Design Sheet to create and list the pros and cons of their and their teammates' designs. Students will discuss their designs with team members and choose one design to use for building their prototype. This design, and reasons why it was chosen, are recorded on the Group Blueprint Design Sheet.

Budget Planning Chart: Any of the lessons can implement a budget for an added mathematical challenge. Prior to the start of the challenge, assign each material a cost and display for the class to reference throughout the challenge. Then decide on an overall budget for the materials. Some lessons may already provide a suggested budget. Students can use the Budget Planning Chart to itemize materials and identify the total cost of the materials needed to complete the challenge. The chart is blank to allow for more flexibility with the materials needed for specific challenges. Ensure students have a limit to what they can spend during the challenge. You can chose not to incorporate a budget if you are short on time. The time needed to assign specific material costs is not included in the overall completion time for the lessons.

Rubric: A rubric for grading the STEAM challenges is included. This rubric focuses on the engineering process. However, it does not include a means to assess the justification components.

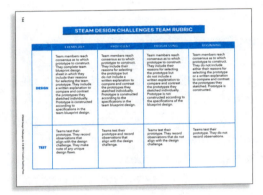

STEAM Job Cards: If your students are struggling with the collaboration process, try assigning them specific roles. Suggestions for jobs are provided on the STEAM Job Cards. Four students per team is recommended. The Accounts Manager role will only occur during the design challenges that involve a budget. In these cases, one student will have two roles, one of which is the Accounts Manager.

STEAM Money: The use of STEAM money is a fun way to engage students and connect the design challenges that incorporate budgets to the real world by having teams "purchase" materials. The use of STEAM money is completely optional. The following suggestions are offered should you choose to incorporate STEAM money into any of your lessons.

- Print multiple copies and laminate for durability and multiple use.

- Enlist the help of a parent volunteer to prepare the STEAM money at the beginning of the year.

- Assign material costs with the class before beginning lessons with budgets, or incorporate this into your long-range planning before school begins. This only has to be done one time. The budget is not set in stone. You may adjust the total budget amount and/or the materials cost according to students' math ability.

Glossary: A glossary of content-related terms has been provided for use as a teacher reference. Or make copies and distribute to students to include in their science notebooks.

THE STANDARDS

SCIENCE
www.nextgenscience.org/search-standards-dci

The Next Generation Science Standards are arranged by disciplinary core ideas (DCI). When accessing these standards, search by standard and DCI. The standards are identified in the lessons by grade level and DCI. (e.g., 5-ESS3-1–Grade 5, Earth and Human Activity, Standard 1).

TECHNOLOGY
www.iste.org/standards

The International Society for Technology in Education (ISTE) publishes the national technology standards. Each of the standards is categorized into four main categories.

1. Creativity and innovation
2. Communication and collaboration
3. Research and information fluency
4. Critical thinking, problem solving, and decision making

Within each of these categories there are more specific indicators that are identified by a letter. Standards within the lessons will be indicated by the category (e.g., ISTE.1).

ENGINEERING
www.nextgenscience.org/search-standards-dci

The Next Generation Science Standards identify the engineering standards as well. They are categorized by the grade band of 3-5 (e.g., 3-5-ETS1-1).

ARTS
www.nationalartsstandards.org
www.corestandards.org/ELA-Literacy

The National Core Arts Standards are divided into four categories:

1. Creating
2. Performing/Presenting/Producing
3. Responding
4. Connecting

Each of these categories contains anchor standards. Within the lesson, the standards will be identified by the category and the anchor standard (e.g., Creating, Anchor Standard #1).

In addition to performance standards, the literacy standards are embedded throughout the lessons. Each lesson identifies specific English language arts (ELA) standards (e.g., CCSS.ELA-LITERACY.W.5.2).

MATH
www.corestandards.org/math

The Common Core Math Standards are divided into two categories:

1. Content
2. Practice

The content standards are those items such as computation and geometry. The practice standards are a framework for ensuring that students are practicing math in a meaningful and appropriate manner.

The content standards will be identified first in the Math Standards column and the Math Practice Standards will be underneath (e.g., CCSS.MATH.CONTENT.5.G.A.2–real world graphing and CCSS.MATH.PRACTICE.MP.4–model with mathematics).

INTEGRATION IN THE ENGINEERING DESIGN CHALLENGE

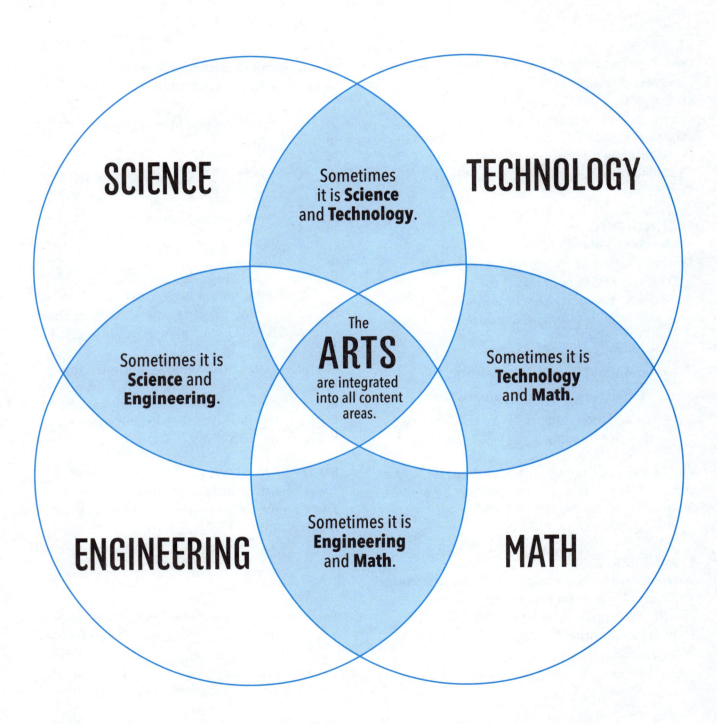

Sometimes it is all five!

STEAM DESIGN PROCESS

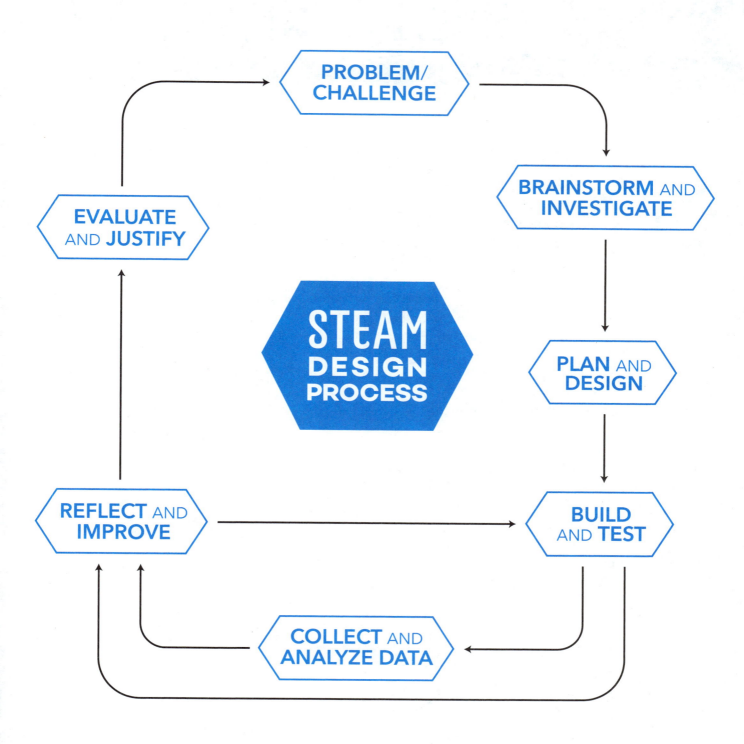

RECORDING INFORMATION IN A SCIENCE NOTEBOOK

Students will record their thinking, answer questions, make observations, and sketch ideas as they work through each design challenge. It is recommended that teachers have students designate a section of their regular science notebooks to these STEAM challenges or have students create a separate STEAM science notebook using a spiral notebook, a composition book, or lined pages stapled together. A generic science notebook cover sheet has been provided in the Appendix.

Have students set up their notebooks based upon the natural breaks in the lesson. Remind students to write the name of the design challenge at the top of the page in their notebooks each time they prepare their notebooks for a new challenge.

Pages 1-3 Background Information

- Students record notes from any information provided by the teacher during whole-group instruction.

- Students record related vocabulary words and their definitions.

- Students record notes from their own independent research, including information gathered through literacy connections and existing background knowledge.

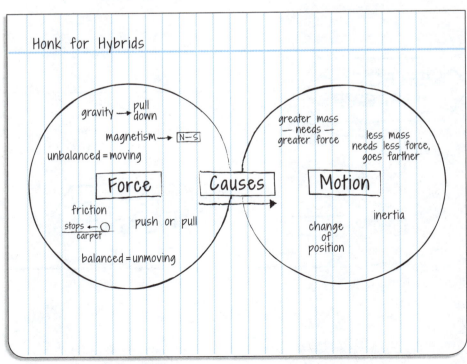

Page 1

Honk for Hybrids
VOCABULARY

force	A push or pull that changes the speed or direction of an object's motion.
motion	The act of changing place or position.
gravity	The force that pulls objects or bodies toward other objects or bodies.
magnetism	Force created by the motion of electric charges. This creates attractive and repulsive forces between objects.
unbalanced forces	Forces of unequal magnitude acting on an object to create acceleration.
balanced forces	Two forces of equal magnitude acting in opposite directions on an object.

Page 2

Honk for Hybrids
NOTES FROM TEXTBOOK

p. 74 — There are many forces that cause motion. Some forces even oppose motion.

p. 75 — A force is a push or pull. Think of a tug-of-war contest, each side pulling the opposite ends of a rope, trying to move the flag and win the contest.

p. 76 — Balanced forces happen when the forces acting on an object are equal and opposite, no movement. In a tug-of-war, the flag doesn't move. Unbalanced force means that one force acting on an object is greater than another force that causes motion.

Page 3

Page 4 Dilemma and Mission

- Display the dilemma and mission for students to record.
- Or make copies of the dilemma and mission for students to glue into their notebooks to use as a reference.

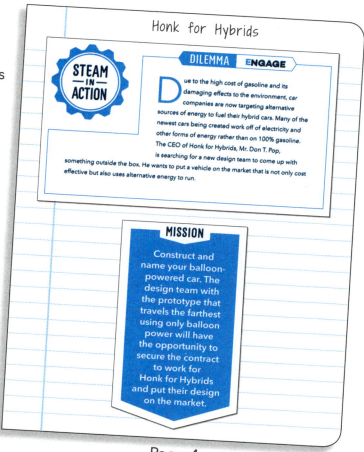

Page 4

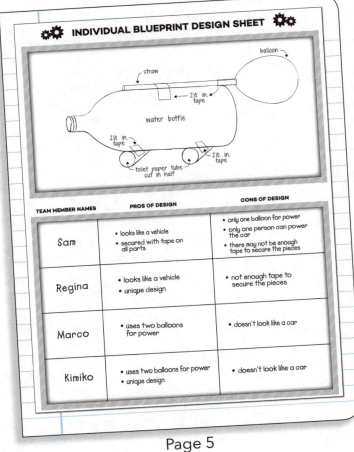

Page 5

Page 5 Blueprint Design

- Students draw their own suggested design. Then students write the pros and cons of both their and their teammates' designs.

- Or make copies of the Individual Blueprint Design Sheet for students to complete and glue into their notebooks.

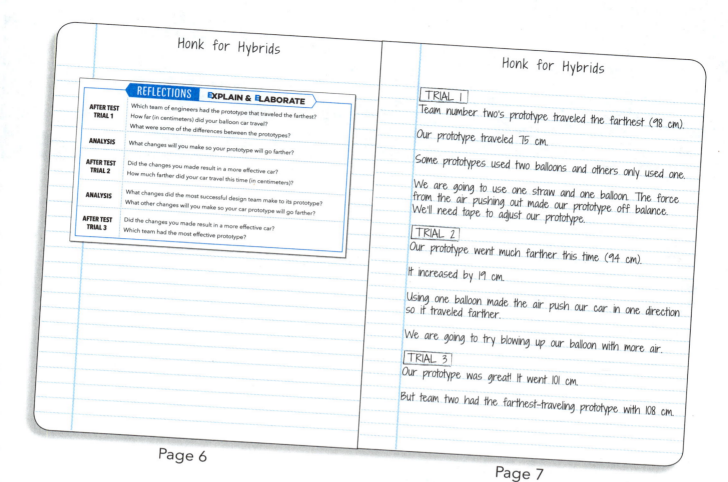

Pages 6-8 Engineering Task, Test Trial, Analyze, Redesign

- Students record analysis questions from the teacher and then record their answers. Or provide copies of the questions for students to glue into their notebooks.

- Record their reflections on the components of the prototypes that were successful and those that were not.

- Include additional pages as needed to allow students to record any notes, observations, and ideas as they construct and test their team prototype.

BLOCK THAT BLIZZARD

STEAM

1-2 HOURS
TIME FOR COMPLETION
TEST TRIALS CAN BE TESTED OVER SEVERAL DAYS

SETTING THE STAGE

DESIGN CHALLENGE PURPOSE

Design a gingerbread house made from graham crackers, following the specifications provided, that will withstand simulated blustery Arctic winds.

TEACHER DEVELOPMENT

Earth has four major systems. They are the **atmosphere** (air), the **geosphere** (land), the **biosphere** (life), and the **hydrosphere** (water). The geosphere, also referred to as the **lithosphere**, consists of soil, sediments, molten rock, and solid rock. The atmosphere contains all of the earth's air. The hydrosphere includes both water and ice. The biosphere is made up of all living things. These systems interact with each other in a multitude of ways that shape and affect the earth's surface and processes. This design challenge focuses on both the atmosphere and the biosphere.

BLOCK THAT BLIZZARD

STUDENT DEVELOPMENT

Introduce the earth's four major systems outlined in the teacher development section. Have students share what they already know about these systems. Tell them that by talking and listening, they have been interacting with each other in order to deepen their understanding of the earth's systems. Explain that the earth's systems interact with each other as well, which results in changes that affect the earth's surface and its processes. For example, the atmosphere and the hydrosphere interact as part of the water cycle. As water is evaporated from the hydrosphere, it becomes a gas and then becomes part of the atmosphere, where it eventually condenses into clouds, becoming part of the hydrosphere again.

Lesson Idea: Write down the earth's four major systems. Assign students to work together in groups of four.

Give each team of students a large piece of construction paper folded into four sections. Assign each student on the team one of the four systems. Give each student on a team a different colored marker representing a different system. Using different colored markers will help you assess individual understanding. Have students discuss the different ways the systems could interact with each other. Next have student use their markers to write the name of their system in one of the sections on the construction paper. Students will take turns drawing arrows from their system to other systems, labeling the arrows with the type of interaction. For example, a student might draw an arrow from the biosphere to the hydrosphere and label it, "Land mammals need fresh water to survive." Collect the papers and check for understanding.

STANDARDS

SCIENCE	TECHNOLOGY	ENGINEERING	ARTS	MATH	ELA
5-ESS2-1	ISTE.1	3-5-ETS1-1	Creating	CCSS.MATH.CONTENT.3.MD.A.2	CCSS.ELA-LITERACY.W.5.3.A
	ISTE.4	3-5-ETS1-2	Anchor Standard #1	CCSS.MATH.PRACTICE.MP2	CCSS.ELA-LITERACY.SL.5.1.C
		3-5-ETS1-3		CCSS.MATH.PRACTICE.MP5	

SCIENCE & ENGINEERING PRACTICES

Developing and Using Models: Develop a model using an example to describe a scientific principle.

Using Mathematics and Computational Thinking: Describe and graph quantities such as area and volume to address scientific questions.

BLOCK THAT BLIZZARD

CROSSCUTTING CONCEPTS

Scale, Proportion, and Quantity: Standard units are used to measure and describe physical quantities such as weight and volume.

Systems and System Models: A system can be described in terms of its components and their interactions.

TARGET VOCABULARY

Arctic
atmosphere
biosphere
environmentalist
geosphere
hydrosphere
shelter

MATERIALS

- graham crackers
- various small candies
- icing
- plastic spoon or knife
- butcher paper or newspaper to cover the workspace
- straws
- tape
- 5 index cards
- ruler
- Testing Materials: fan or hair dryer for the whole classroom

LITERACY CONNECTIONS

Extreme Weather: Surviving Tornadoes, Sandstorms, Hailstorms, Blizzards, Hurricanes, and More! by Thomas M. Kostigen

NOTES

BLOCK THAT BLIZZARD

DILEMMA — ENGAGE

Frigid Frank has just returned from his now famous trek across the Arctic Circle. Upon his return, he shared with his coworkers that the worst part of his trip was when he had to find shelter, especially when the Arctic winds picked up. Frigid Frank would like to go on another Arctic trek and mentioned that it would be nice to have a shelter to protect him from the harsh elements.

Wintery Wanda, head environmentalist of Winter Wonderland Incorporated, mentioned Frigid Frank's dilemma to her teams of engineers. She asked them to design an environmentally friendly shelter for Frigid Frank and his crew to use while on their Arctic Circle trek. Each of the teams' prototypes must follow the special guidelines listed in the Mission section. She reminded the teams that the shelter they build must be able to stand on its own for at least 30 seconds in simulated Arctic wind.

MISSION

Create a structure out of graham crackers that is at least 15 in. tall, has 500 g of candy used in the design of the structure, and remains standing through an "Arctic blast" (a 30-second blast of air from a fan or hair dryer). Will your team of engineers be able to protect Frigid Frank and his crew on their next trek to the Arctic Circle?

BLUEPRINT — EXPLORE

Provide the Individual and Group Blueprint Design Sheets to engineering teams. Have individual students sketch a prototype to present to the other members of their team. Team members will discuss the pros and cons of each sketch and then select one prototype to construct.

BLOCK THAT BLIZZARD

 ENGINEERING TASK **TEST TRIAL** **ANALYZE** **REDESIGN**

ENGINEERING TASK	TEST TRIAL	ANALYZE	REDESIGN
Each team will construct a graham cracker structure prototype.	Each team will test its prototype by placing it in front of an "Arctic blast" from the fan or hair dryer for 30 seconds to see if it can withstand the harsh "Arctic winds."	Facilitate analytical discussions comparing the design and structure of the prototype of each team. Allow teams to reflect on their designs and compare them to other teams' prototypes.	Allow teams to redesign their prototypes if necessary, including altering the original sketches on the Group Blueprint Design Sheet using a colored pencil to show the changes they have made. The goal is to design a more effective prototype.

HELPFUL TIPS

- After the Test Trial, have teams take a gallery walk to view other teams' designs for possible ideas to assist them in the Analyze and Redesign portions of the engineering design process.

- If teams are successful on the first try, encourage them to make their prototypes even more efficient. If it is a scenario in which this is not feasible, distribute team members to other teams to be a support for them in making their prototypes more efficient. Alternatively, at teacher discretion, move students on to the Justification portion of the lesson.

- If after the third test the final prototype is still unsuccessful, have students write how they would start over. These challenges are meant to have students build on what they originally designed. If the design proved to be unsuccessful, encourage a reflection or justification on what they would do if they were allowed to start again from scratch.

BLOCK THAT BLIZZARD

REFLECTIONS — EXPLAIN & ELABORATE

AFTER TEST TRIAL 1
- What parts of the structure stayed standing?
- Which portions did not withstand the "Arctic wind"?

ANALYSIS
- Which team of engineers had the most effective prototype?
- Did a certain design feature make a difference?
- What changes, if any, will your team make to your prototype?

AFTER TEST TRIAL 2
- Did the changes increase the sturdiness of your structure?
- Did the changes make your structure weaker?
- What do you need to change to make your structure stronger?

ANALYSIS
- What changes did other teams make to increase the strength of their structures?
- What new changes will you make to your prototype?

AFTER TEST TRIAL 3
- What happened differently this time?
- Did your structure withstand the "Arctic wind" more effectively?
- Explain why you think these changes helped your structure withstand the "Arctic wind."

JUSTIFICATION — EVALUATE

TECHNOLOGY
A. Create a blog to document the creation of the graham cracker structure to protect Frigid Frank and his team from a blizzard.
B. Create a videotaped journal entry to send to Wintery Wanda describing what steps they took to create the graham cracker structure.

ELA
Write journal entries from the perspective of Frigid Frank. Include descriptions of the weather conditions and how he found the resources to create the structure the engineers want him to construct to protect himself from the "Arctic wind." Think about the actual natural materials that the prototype materials represented in the challenge.

ARTS
Create a skit in which you are the weathercaster that Frigid Frank watched on TV prior to going on his expedition to the Arctic Circle.

I CAN SEE CLEARLY NOW

STEAm

2-3 HOURS
TIME FOR COMPLETION

DESIGN CHALLENGE PURPOSE

Design and construct a water filter that will purify the polluted water sample to make it clear enough to read an eye chart through.

TEACHER DEVELOPMENT

Over 97% of the earth's water is salt water. The water found at the earth's surface in lakes, rivers, streams, ponds, and swamps makes up only 3% of the world's freshwater. Nearly 70% of that freshwater is frozen in the icecaps of Antarctica and Greenland. Most of the remainder is present as soil moisture, or lies in deep underground **aquifers** as groundwater not accessible for human use. Only about 1% of the world's freshwater is accessible for direct human use. This is the water found in lakes, rivers, reservoirs, and underground sources. This amount is regularly renewed by rain and snowfall and is, therefore, available on a sustainable basis. Water pollution is a serious issue. In developing countries, 70% of industrial wastes are dumped into waters, polluting the usable water supply. Approximately 3.6 million people die from diseases related to water pollution each year.

I CAN SEE CLEARLY NOW

STUDENT DEVELOPMENT

In order to complete this challenge, students must have an understanding of the availability of fresh, drinkable water. They also need to understand the meaning of the vocabulary terms related to this design challenge.

Lesson Idea: A great way to demonstrate this idea to students is to model the earth's water supply using beakers. Begin by asking students what percentage of the world's water they think is fresh, drinkable water. Let them discuss and then come to a general consensus as a class. Write this percentage number on the board. Pour 100 ml of water into a beaker. Add 2-3 drops of blue food coloring to make it more visible to students. Explain that this represents all of the water in the world. Pour 97 ml from the first beaker into an empty beaker. Hold up the beaker with 97 ml of water for students to see. Inform students that this beaker represents the oceans. State that this water is not drinkable because it is salt water. Set it aside. Hold up the first beaker that is now left with 3 ml of water, and explain that this represents the amount of freshwater in the world. Take a pipette and fill it up. Hold up what is left in the beaker representing freshwater. Explain that this freshwater is not available for drinking because it is part of the polar ice caps and glaciers in the North and South Poles. Hold up the pipette filled with water. Ask students if this seems like a lot of water for all the living creatures on our planet. Then explain we have even less than that. Talk to students about how water becomes polluted. Tell students the design challenge is about helping to solve that problem.

STANDARDS

SCIENCE	TECHNOLOGY	ENGINEERING	ARTS	MATH	ELA
5-ESS2-2	ISTE.1	3-5-ETS1-1	Creating	CCSS.MATH.PRACTICE.MP5	CCSS.ELA-LITERACY.W.5.7
		3-5-ETS1-2	Anchor Standard #1	CCSS.MATH.PRACTICE.MP6	CCSS.ELA-LITERACY.RI.5.9
		3-5-ETS1-3	Anchor Standard #2		

SCIENCE & ENGINEERING PRACTICES

Asking Questions and Defining Problems: Define a simple design problem that can be solved through the development of an object, tool, process, or system and includes several criteria for success and constraints on material, time, or cost.

Developing and Using Models: Develop a model using an example to describe a scientific principle.

I CAN SEE CLEARLY NOW

CROSSCUTTING CONCEPTS

Scale, Proportion, and Quantity: Standard units are used to measure and describe physical quantities such as weight and volume.

Systems and System Models: A system can be described in terms of its components and their interactions.

TARGET VOCABULARY

- aquifer
- clarity
- freshwater
- natural resource
- pollution
- water quality

MATERIALS

Filter (container): 16 oz. water bottle with bottom cut off (every team gets one)

Filter materials:
- paper towels
- pebbles
- rocks
- sand
- aquarium charcoal
- coffee filter
- cotton balls
- marbles

Testing Materials:
- eye chart (page 129)
- rubric (page 130)
- stock certificate (page 131)
- clear plastic cups
- bucket of polluted water (Use muddy water with lots of sediment. Remember to save enough water for the retest.)

LITERACY CONNECTIONS

Ryan and Jimmy: And the Well in Africa That Brought Them Together by Herb Shoveller

NOTES

I CAN SEE CLEARLY NOW

DILEMMA — ENGAGE

Currently, there is a global competition for natural resources such as drinkable water. The company Needwater Inc. is looking for ways to turn polluted water into safe drinking water to meet the ever-increasing demand for safe water. Needwater Inc. is looking for a filter that produces the best quality of drinkable water. The company will award the team of engineers that builds the most successful filter with a 5% share of the company's stock. Your filter must purify 200 ml of polluted water. The clarity of the water will be tested by how easy it is to read an eye chart through the water.

MISSION

Construct a filter that produces water clear enough that someone can read the smallest line on the eye chart through it.

BLUEPRINT — EXPLORE

Provide the Individual and Group Blueprint Design Sheets to engineering teams. Have individual students sketch a prototype to present to the other members of their team. Team members will discuss the pros and cons of each sketch and then select one prototype to construct.

I CAN SEE CLEARLY NOW

 ENGINEERING TASK

Each team will construct a water filter prototype.

 TEST TRIAL

Teams will test their filters using the polluted water, pouring their filtered water sample into the clear plastic cups, and then using the mini eye chart to examine water clarity.

 ANALYZE

Each team member should read the eye chart through the filtered water and rate the sample's clarity using the rubric provided.

Students must record their results and explain what happened.

Each team member must record his or her own clarity assessment rating. Then the team will use the scores to determine the team's mean (average).

 REDESIGN

After analyzing their data, student teams review their original design. Teams then make adjustments by altering the original sketch using a colored pencil to show the changes they have made. The goal is to improve their prototypes for the next trial.

HELPFUL TIPS

- After the Test Trial, have teams take a gallery walk to view other teams' designs for possible ideas to assist them in the Analyze and Redesign portions of the engineering design process.

- If teams are successful on the first try, encourage them to make their prototypes even more efficient. If it is a scenario in which this is not feasible, distribute team members to other teams to be a support for them in making their prototypes more efficient. Alternatively, at teacher discretion, move students on to the Justification portion of the lesson.

- If after the third test the final prototype is still unsuccessful, have students write how they would start over. These challenges are meant to have students build on what they originally designed. If the design proved to be unsuccessful, encourage a reflection or justification on what they would do if they were allowed to start again from scratch.

I CAN SEE CLEARLY NOW

REFLECTIONS — EXPLAIN & ELABORATE

AFTER TEST TRIAL 1	What rating did you give your water sample? What was the team mean (average) for the rating of the team water sample? If there was more than a 2-point difference between your rating and the average, how do you explain the difference?
ANALYSIS	What do you think you should do to improve the clarity of your water sample? What changes did your team make to the blueprint design?
AFTER TEST TRIAL 2	What rating did you give your water sample? What was the team mean (average) for the rating of the team water sample? If there was more than a 2-point difference between your rating and the average, how do you explain the difference?
ANALYSIS	What do you think you should do to improve the clarity of your water sample? What changes did your team make to the blueprint design?
AFTER TEST TRIAL 3	What rating did you give your water sample? What was the team mean (average) for the rating of the team water sample? If there was more than a 2-point difference between your rating and the average, how do you explain the difference?

JUSTIFICATION — EVALUATE

TECHNOLOGY	Create a slide show presentation with a proposal for your final prototype. In addition to your proposal, the slide show should include examples of polluted US waters and natural and man-made methods of purification, such as aquifers. Use the Internet to research articles and sources to support the information in the slide show. Cite all sources.
ELA	Complete a reflection paragraph that answers the following question: What did you learn about the impact (good and/or bad) that humans have had on water quality?
ARTS	Use a large sheet of butcher paper to create a billboard advertisement for your prototype on how it will change the world. Include a slogan and name for your prototype.

PLEASE RAIN ON MY PARADE

STEAM

SETTING THE STAGE

DESIGN CHALLENGE PURPOSE
Create a device to collect and conserve the most rainwater.

TEACHER DEVELOPMENT

The **water cycle** (and all of the earth's living organisms dependence on it) is an example of how the earth's major systems (the atmosphere, the hydrosphere, the geosphere, and biosphere) interact. The sun's energy powers the water cycle. Because it is a cycle, there is no real beginning or end. For a demonstration to students, it is often most feasible to describe the water cycle from the perspective of one drop of water. Since 97% of the earth's water can be found in the oceans, that is a good place to begin. The one drop of water is in an ocean that is part of the hydrosphere. The sun's energy heats the water and causes the one drop of water to become a gas, which causes it to rise into the atmosphere. The process of liquid water becoming a gas is called **evaporation**. As the drop of water cools in the atmosphere, it turns back into a liquid. This process is called **condensation**. The clouds in the sky are the liquid water molecules coming together. So now our one drop of water is in a cloud. When the water in the clouds become heavy and dense, they start to fall from the atmosphere. This is called **precipitation**. There are four types of precipitation. They are rain, sleet, snow, and hail. Now our one drop of water is falling as precipitation. It could fall back into the ocean, or winds could carry the clouds over land, lakes, forests, or towns. Precipitation falls in uneven patterns. What is considered normal for a particular area is what has been averaged over a number of years. A **drought** happens when there is considerably less than normal amounts of precipitation over a period of time, causing water-related problems for the area.

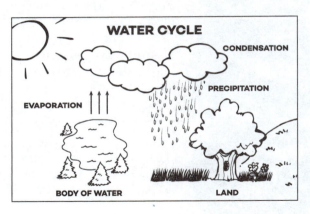

PLEASE RAIN ON MY PARADE

STUDENT DEVELOPMENT

Students will need a basic understanding of the vocabulary associated with this challenge. When students have background knowledge of ways to collect water, they can apply that knowledge when they design their prototype. A working knowledge of the relationship between absorption, reflection, and colors is important and will lead students in an interesting direction when designing their prototypes. Knowing how the water cycle works, especially evaporation, is an advantage for this activity.

Lesson Idea: Have students draw and label a water cycle diagram as a quick review. Conduct the following simple demonstration activity to teach absorption and reflection. Fill three beakers or cups with water. Record the temperature in all three cups and write that on the board. Leave one cup uncovered and make a cover for each of the other beakers. One cover should be a light color and the other cover should be dark. Cut the paper covers so that a small amount of the paper will fold over the top of the beakers. Use a rubber band to hold the paper onto the beakers. Take and record the temperatures in the beakers. Place the beakers outside in the sun for one hour. Take and record the temperature of the water in the three beakers after one hour. Have students compare and discuss the temperature results. They should find that the darker color has the highest temperature.

STANDARDS

SCIENCE	TECHNOLOGY	ENGINEERING	ARTS	MATH	ELA
5-ESS2-1	ISTE.1	3-5-ETS1-1	Creating	CCSS.MATH.CONTENT.5.MD.B.2	CCSS.ELA-LITERACY.W.5.2
	ISTE.4	3-5-ETS1-2	Anchor Standard #1	CCSS.MATH.PRACTICE.MP2	
		3-5-ETS1-3		CCSS.MATH.PRACTICE.MP5	

SCIENCE & ENGINEERING PRACTICES

Developing and Using Models: Develop a model using an example to describe a scientific principle.

Using Mathematics and Computational Thinking: Describe and graph quantities such as area and volume to address scientific questions.

PLEASE RAIN ON MY PARADE

CROSSCUTTING CONCEPTS

Scale, Proportion, and Quantity: Standard units are used to measure and describe physical quantities such as weight and volume.

Systems and System Models: A system can be described in terms of its components and their interactions.

TARGET VOCABULARY

- absorption
- atmosphere
- biosphere
- drought
- evaporation
- geosphere
- hydrosphere
- precipitation
- rain barrel
- reflection
- reservoir
- temperature
- water demand

MATERIALS

- cleaned soup cans with smooth edges
- clear and colored plastic cups or recycled containers
- colored paper
- graduated cylinders
- tape
- watering can to represent rain (students add water to can)

LITERACY CONNECTIONS

The Legend of the Bluebonnet by Tomie dePaola

NOTES

PLEASE RAIN ON MY PARADE

DILEMMA — ENGAGE

Governor Guzzletown is worried about his state. There is a severe drought going on, and no one is taking it seriously. The plants are starting to die, the lakes and ponds are low, and there seems to be no end in sight. There have been occasional rainstorms. However, the rain quickly dries up when it hits the dry soil, so water restrictions are a must. The people of the state are adjusting to the new water restrictions, but their lawns are turning brown, and water used for washing is being limited.

Governor Guzzletown has decided to create a contest to see who can create the best device to collect and conserve water to use for washing and watering lawns. The winning prototype will be featured in the Guzzletown News and will be advertised everywhere.

MISSION

Create a device to collect and conserve the most rainwater.

BLUEPRINT — EXPLORE

Provide the Individual and Group Blueprint Design Sheets to engineering teams. Have individual students sketch a prototype to present to the other members of their team. Team members will discuss the pros and cons of each sketch and then select one prototype to construct.

PLEASE RAIN ON MY PARADE

 ENGINEERING TASK → **TEST TRIAL** → **ANALYZE** → **REDESIGN**

ENGINEERING TASK	TEST TRIAL	ANALYZE	REDESIGN
Each team will construct a rainwater collection prototype.	Teams will test by pouring 100 ml of water into a watering can. Teacher will pour water over their prototypes. Measure remaining water after three days. (Prototypes should be left in area that receives direct sunlight if possible.)	After three days, students will carefully measure the amount of water that is left in their prototype and record their results. (The teacher may want to pour so that there are no accidents to skew the results.) The teacher should keep a class data chart of the results so that groups can compare the other teams' results to their own.	Teams can then redesign their prototypes for retesting. All teams will measure another 100 ml of water. Teacher will pour water over their prototypes. Measure remaining water after three days.

HELPFUL TIPS

- After the Test Trial, have teams take a gallery walk to view other teams' designs for possible ideas to assist them in the Analyze and Redesign portions of the engineering design process.

- If teams are successful on the first try, encourage them to make their prototypes even more efficient. If it is a scenario in which this is not feasible, distribute team members to other teams to be a support for them in making their prototypes more efficient. Alternatively, at teacher discretion, move students on to the Justification portion of the lesson.

- If after the third test the final prototype is still unsuccessful, have students write how they would start over. These challenges are meant to have students build on what they originally designed. If the design proved to be unsuccessful, encourage a reflection or justification on what they would do if they were allowed to start again from scratch.

PLEASE RAIN ON MY PARADE

REFLECTIONS — EXPLAIN & ELABORATE

AFTER TEST TRIAL 1	How much evaporation did each team have?
ANALYSIS	Which team of engineers had the most effective prototype? Have teams discuss the results to determine why the design that had the most water left fared better than the rest? Suggest teams determine one variable to change in order to see improvement.
AFTER TEST TRIAL 2	What changes did the teams make to improve their results? Did the color or type of material create a better result?
ANALYSIS	Make sure that teams understand which variable caused the positive changes in their design. Review the need to only change one variable in order to determine a better design.
AFTER TEST TRIAL 3	What teams had positive results from changing a variable and what teams did not? Ask the teams which color or material worked best and why they believe it improved their design.

JUSTIFICATION — EVALUATE

TECHNOLOGY	Use the website http://droughtmonitor.unl.edu/ to gather real-time data to compare the area you live in to earlier weeks or years. Then create a climate forecast that you can use to present for a weather broadcast. Use your prototype as a prop, and explain why it would help the area that you live in.
ELA	Write a persuasive essay to Governor Guzzletown to convince him to choose your team's prototype. Use details from your prototype to make your case.
ARTS	Create a drawing or 3-D model of your prototype that can be used as a marketing tool to promote your product.

STELLAR SUNDIALS

DESIGN CHALLENGE PURPOSE

Design and construct a sundial that accurately tells time to the nearest hour.

TEACHER DEVELOPMENT

When the earth rotates on its axis, the sun appears to move across the sky, causing objects to cast **shadows**. A **sundial** is a device that uses the sun to tell time. Most sundials have two basic components: A **gnomon**, or pointer, casts a shadow and a numbered dial is used to show which hour the shadow falls on. Sundials come in all shapes and sizes. However, the most popular is a flat, circular shape.

STELLAR SUNDIALS

STUDENT DEVELOPMENT

In order to complete this challenge, students must have an understanding of the patterns of daily changes in the length and direction of shadows during the day, from sunrise to sunset. Students must have a working knowledge of how to collect data in order to be able to display it graphically. Students may draw upon their previous learning of line plots and bar graphs. Students must be familiar with using measurement tools to measure distances.

Lesson Idea: Students should research information regarding what sundials were used for throughout history and what the differences in lengths of shadows can tell us about time. You may also want to do the following simple activity involving shadows. Place students into groups of four, and have them find a spot around the room about four feet from a wall. Give each team a flashlight and a box of small objects (e.g., paperclip, toy car, pencil, and dry erase marker). Then dim the lights. Three of the students in each group should be sitting facing the wall. The fourth student in each group will stand behind the others, shining the flashlight on the wall. This student will hold one object at a time in front of the flashlight, casting a shadow on the wall. The students that are sitting will try to guess what the object is from its shadow. Ensure students try moving it closer and farther from the flashlight to see its effect on the shadow.

STANDARDS

SCIENCE	TECHNOLOGY	ENGINEERING	ARTS	MATH	ELA
5-ESS1-2	ISTE.1	3-5-ETS1-1	Creating	CCSS.MATH.PRACTICE.MP4	CCSS.ELA-LITERACY.W.5.1
	ISTE.4	3-5-ETS1-2	Anchor Standard #1		CCSS.ELA-LITERACY.SL.5.5
		3-5-ETS1-3			CCSS.ELA-LITERACY.SL.5.1.C

SCIENCE & ENGINEERING PRACTICES

Analyzing and Interpreting Data: Represent data in graphic displays (bar graphs, pictographs, and/or pie charts) to reveal patterns that indicate relationships.

STELLAR SUNDIALS

CROSSCUTTING CONCEPTS

Patterns: Similarities and differences in patterns can be used to sort, classify, communicate, and analyze simple rates of change for natural phenomena.

TARGET VOCABULARY

- gnomon
- shadow
- sundial

MATERIALS

- 1 cup of modeling clay
- cereal boxes
- chalk
- measuring tape
- paper plates
- craft sticks
- rocks
- straws
- washers
- ruler
- watch or clock

LITERACY CONNECTIONS

On Earth
by G. Brian Karas

NOTES

STELLAR SUNDIALS

DILEMMA — ENGAGE

Your team has been chosen to compete on the reality TV show called *Tick Tock*. The competition begins when you are dropped off by plane in a remote area, your location unknown. You are left with nothing but clothes and food to last your team three days. Over the course of four weeks, you will be asked to complete various tasks in competition with three other teams. The first task you are faced with is creating some sort of device to help you track time while you are living in this remote area. There is a supply drop-off zone about two miles from your living area, and items will be dropped there every other day at 3:00 p.m. Since you will be completing various tasks with your teammates during this competition, it is important that you do not waste much time sending members to collect supplies.

MISSION

Create a sundial that will tell time accurately to the nearest hour.

BLUEPRINT — EXPLORE

Provide the Individual and Group Blueprint Design Sheets to engineering teams. Have individual students sketch a prototype to present to the other members of their team. Team members will discuss the pros and cons of each sketch and then select one prototype to construct.

STELLAR SUNDIALS

ENGINEERING TASK

Each team will construct a sundial prototype.

Prototypes will need to be set up outside in an area that gets sunlight all day.

TEST TRIAL

Teams will test their prototypes and record their observations. Students should record the time reading on their sundial. They should discuss their accuracy after tracking and marking time each hour. Students will need to go outside at least three times on the first day.

ANALYZE

Teams will analyze the results of the test and determine the causes for what they observed.

REDESIGN

After analyzing their data, student teams will go back to their submitted designs and make adjustments. They will alter the original sketches using a colored pencil to show the changes they have made. The goal is to improve their prototypes for the next trial.

💡 HELPFUL TIPS 💡

- After the Test Trial, have teams take a gallery walk to view other teams' designs for possible ideas to assist them in the Analyze and Redesign portions of the engineering design process.

- If teams are successful on the first try, encourage them to make their prototypes even more efficient. If it is a scenario in which this is not feasible, distribute team members to other teams to be a support for them in making their prototypes more efficient. Alternatively, at teacher discretion, move students on to the Justification portion of the lesson.

- If after the third test the final prototype is still unsuccessful, have students write how they would start over. These challenges are meant to have students build on what they originally designed. If the design proved to be unsuccessful, encourage a reflection or justification on what they would do if they were allowed to start again from scratch.

STELLAR SUNDIALS

REFLECTIONS — EXPLAIN & ELABORATE

AFTER TEST TRIAL 1	Which team of engineers had the most effective prototype? Were you able to tell time accurately? Measure, record, and plot on a graph the length of your shadow.
ANALYSIS	What were the differences between the prototypes with the most accurate time calculations and the least accurate time calculations? What adjustments do you need to make in order to make your sundial more accurate?
AFTER TEST TRIAL 2	Which team of engineers had the most effective prototype? Were you able to track time accurately after your adjustments? What changes did you include that made your design more effective? Measure, record, and plot on a graph the length of your shadow.
ANALYSIS	What were the differences between the prototypes with the most accurate and least accurate sundials? How do you know? What other adjustments do you want to make to your sundial to increase accuracy?
AFTER TEST TRIAL 3	Which team of engineers had the most effective prototype? What changes did you include that made your design more effective? Measure, record, and plot on a graph the length of your shadow.

JUSTIFICATION — EVALUATE

TECHNOLOGY	Create a slideshow presentation to promote your product. Include a graph representing the measurements of the lengths of your shadows compared to that of your competition. Also include background information about your prototype and directions for construction.
ELA	Write a letter to the producers of *Tick Tock* explaining why your product was the most successful.
MATH	Create math problems related to time for others to complete. For example, how much time passed between your first trial and your last? In the first trial, what was the time difference between the most accurate and the least accurate sundials?

BUILD A BETTER BRIDGE
STEAM

1½-2 HOURS
TIME FOR COMPLETION

DESIGN CHALLENGE PURPOSE

Build a bridge that spans a distance of 30 cm and holds a minimum mass of 500 mg for 10 seconds.

TEACHER DEVELOPMENT

Force is a push or a pull. Students will be building a bridge that must overcome the force of **gravity**. Gravity is a force of attraction between objects. The greater the mass of an object, the greater the pull of attraction between the object and the earth. Because the earth has so much mass, we are all attracted, or pulled, toward its center. We exert force through our muscles to resist the pull of gravity. Movement is a change in position of an object. When an object is stationary, the forces acting on it are **balanced**. When the object moves, then the forces acting on it are **unbalanced**. Think of a tug-of-war contest. When both sides are applying equal force, the rope doesn't move. If one side pulls the rope with greater force than the other team, the rope moves toward the team pulling it the hardest.

BUILD A BETTER BRIDGE

STUDENT DEVELOPMENT

Students need to understand that the force of gravity will be acting on their bridge. They must build a structure that will use the force of the desk or table pushing against their structure to balance with the force of gravity pulling it down.

Lesson Idea: Desktop Air Hockey! Have students work in pairs. Each pair will need one ping-pong ball and two straws. Line the sides of a student desk with textbooks, leaving a small space about 5 in. wide on opposite ends of the desk for the goal area. Place the ball in the center of the desk. Have students stand at opposite ends of the desk, in front of the open space, and blow air through the straw to push the ball across the table and into their opponent's goal. After they've had time to play, discuss what they observed. This activity shows how force moves an object. Talk about how the forces acting on the ball were balanced, or equal, when it didn't move.

STANDARDS

SCIENCE	TECHNOLOGY	ENGINEERING	ARTS	MATH	ELA
5-PS2-1		3-5-ETS1-1	Creating	CCSS.MATH.PRACTICE.MP4	CCSS.ELA-LITERACY.W.5.2
		3-5-ETS1-2	Anchor Standard #1	CCSS.MATH.PRACTICE.MP5	CCSS.ELA-LITERACY.SL.5.1.C
		3-5-ETS1-3			

SCIENCE & ENGINEERING PRACTICES

Asking Questions and Defining Problems: Define a simple design problem that can be solved through the development of an object, tool, process, or system and includes several criteria for success and constraints on materials, time, or cost.

Planning and Carrying Out Investigations: Plan and conduct an investigation collaboratively to produce data to serve as the basis for evidence, using fair tests in which variables are controlled and the number of trials considered.

Constructing Explanations and Designing Solutions: Generate and compare multiple solutions to a problem based on how well they meet the criteria and constraints of the design problem.

BUILD A BETTER BRIDGE

CROSSCUTTING CONCEPTS

Influence of Engineering, Technology, and Science on Society and the Natural World: People's needs and wants change over time, as do their demands for new and improved technologies.

TARGET VOCABULARY

balanced force

gravity

load

mass

span

unbalanced force

MATERIALS

Bridge:
- straws (maximum of 25 per bridge)
- string
- masking tape
- scissors
- container for holding load (such as a paper cup or plastic bag)
- timer

Load:
- marbles (or use metal weights, sand, or water in a container)
- scale (spring scales are perfect for this) for measuring the mass of the load
- permit (page 132)

LITERACY CONNECTIONS

Famous Bridges of the World: Measuring Length, Weight, and Volume by Yolonda Maxwell

NOTES

BUILD A BETTER BRIDGE

DILEMMA — ENGAGE

The town of Bridgeville boasts of its many beautiful bridges. However, many of them have been closed for repair or replacement. The bridges were built when people still used a horse and buggy to travel; therefore, they can't hold the load of today's motorcycles, cars, and trucks. The town's civil engineers have noticed this is a huge problem, and that's why they closed the bridges. Bridgeville needs your help! The town council needs you to design and construct a prototype of a new bridge to help them get their traffic flowing smoothly again.

MISSION

Build a bridge that can span a distance of 30 cm and hold a load of 500 mg for a minimum of 10 seconds. Will your team of civil engineers win a building permit and seal of approval from the Bridgeville town council?

BLUEPRINT — EXPLORE

Provide the Individual and Group Blueprint Design Sheets to engineering teams. Have individual students sketch a prototype to present to the other members of their team. Team members will discuss the pros and cons of each sketch and then select one prototype to construct.

BUILD A BETTER BRIDGE

ENGINEERING TASK

Each team will build a bridge that spans a distance of 30 cm and holds a load of 500 mg for a minimum of 10 seconds.

TEST TRIAL

Teams will build and test their bridges. Each bridge must span a distance of 30 cm. Students will hang a load from the bridge using a paper cup or plastic bag containing a mass equal to 500 mg. It must hold the load for 10 seconds.

Note: The teacher should pause engineering teams so they can observe when a team tests its bridge by adding a load.

ANALYZE

Students must record their results, explain what happened, and share their reasoning.

REDESIGN

Students will return to their designs and use a colored pencil to make changes based on their observations and explanation.

HELPFUL TIPS

- After the Test Trial, have teams take a gallery walk to view other teams' designs for possible ideas to assist them in the Analyze and Redesign portions of the engineering design process.

- If teams are successful on the first try, encourage them to make their prototypes even more efficient. If it is a scenario in which this is not feasible, distribute team members to other teams to be a support for them in making their prototypes more efficient. Alternatively, at teacher discretion, move students on to the Justification portion of the lesson.

- If after the third test the final prototype is still unsuccessful, have students write how they would start over. These challenges are meant to have students build on what they originally designed. If the design proved to be unsuccessful, encourage a reflection or justification on what they would do if they were allowed to start again from scratch.

BUILD A BETTER BRIDGE

REFLECTIONS — EXPLAIN & ELABORATE

AFTER TEST TRIAL 1
Which team of engineers had the most effective bridge prototype?
What were the differences between the prototypes?
Did certain design features make a difference?

ANALYSIS
What changes can you make to your prototype that will make your prototype more successful?

AFTER TEST TRIAL 2
Which team of engineers had the most effective bridge prototype?
Did the changes you made to your prototype improve your success?
What were the differences between your first and second prototypes?

ANALYSIS
What changes can you make to your prototype that will make your prototype more successful?

AFTER TEST TRIAL 3
Which team of engineers had the most effective prototype?
What were the differences between your prototype and the other teams' prototypes?

JUSTIFICATION — EVALUATE

ARTS
Create a drawing (blueprint) of your bridge. Include labels and the name of the bridge.

ELA
Write a report to the Bridgeville town council that includes a summary of the design challenge process. Start by stating the problem and going step by step through each stage of the process (e.g., design, test, redesign, and retest). Include the materials used to construct the prototype and a description of the load used to test the bridge.

HONK FOR HYBRIDS

STEAM

1-2 HOURS TIME FOR COMPLETION

DESIGN CHALLENGE PURPOSE

Design a prototype of a balloon-powered car that will travel as far as possible.

TEACHER DEVELOPMENT

This engineering challenge uses science content knowledge from third and fourth grade. Students should have background knowledge of force and motion. **Force** is defined as a push or a pull. Force causes motion. **Motion** occurs when an object changes position or location. Other types of forces include gravity, friction, and magnetism. **Friction** is the force resisting motion between objects that slide against each other. Objects must touch to create friction. **Gravity** is the force of attraction between objects with mass. The earth has great mass so we are pulled toward its center.

HONK FOR HYBRIDS

STUDENT DEVELOPMENT

Review force and motion with your students. Place students into groups of four. Give each group four straws, a tennis ball, and a ping-pong ball. Have students place the ping-pong ball in the middle of the table. Tell them to leave the ball there for 30 seconds or more. Discuss their observations. They should note that the ball didn't move. Discuss **Newton's first law of motion**: an object at rest will stay at rest unless a force acts upon it. The second part of Newton's first law is that an object in motion will stay in motion unless a force acts upon it. Tell them they need to move the ball without directly touching it. Discuss what they did and what they observed. Repeat this activity with the tennis ball. Students should note that it takes a greater amount of force to move the tennis ball. This demonstrates **Newton's second law of motion**: The greater the mass of an object, the greater amount of force needed to move it. Next, have them demonstrate **Newton's third law of motion** by rolling two tennis balls toward each other. Discuss their observations. They should note that for every action, there is an equal and opposite reaction.

STANDARDS

SCIENCE	TECHNOLOGY	ENGINEERING	ARTS	MATH	ELA
3-PS2-1	ISTE.2	3-5-ETS1-1	Creating	CCSS.MATH.CONTENT.5.NBT.B.7	CCSS.ELA-LITERACY.W.5.2
4-PS3-3		3-5-ETS1-2	Anchor Standard #1	CCSS.MATH.CONTENT.5.MD.A.1	CCSS.ELA-LITERACY.SL.5.1.C
		3-5-ETS1-3	Performing		
			Anchor Standard #5		

SCIENCE & ENGINEERING PRACTICES

Asking Questions and Defining Problems: Define a simple design problem that can be solved through the development of an object, tool, process, or system and includes several criteria for success and constraints on materials, time, or cost.

Planning and Carrying Out Investigations: Plan and conduct an investigation collaboratively to produce data to serve as the basis for evidence, using fair tests in which variables are controlled and the number of trials considered.

Constructing Explanations and Designing Solutions: Generate and compare multiple solutions to a problem based on how well they meet the criteria and constraints of the design problem.

HONK FOR HYBRIDS

CROSSCUTTING CONCEPTS

Influence of Engineering, Technology, and Science on Society and the Natural World: People's needs and wants change over time, as do their demands for new and improved technologies.

Engineers improve existing technologies or develop new ones to increase their benefits, decrease known risks, and meet societal demands.

TARGET VOCABULARY

acceleration
force
motion
Newton's Laws of Motion
speed

MATERIALS

- balloons
- straws
- rubber bands
- masking tape
- water bottle
- toilet paper tube
- ruler

LITERACY CONNECTIONS

All About Electric and Hybrid Cars and Who's Driving Them by Stephanie Bearce

NOTES

HONK FOR HYBRIDS

DILEMMA — ENGAGE

Due to the high cost of gasoline and its damaging effects to the environment, car companies are now targeting alternative sources of energy to fuel their hybrid cars. Many of the newest cars being created work off of electricity and other forms of energy rather than on 100% gasoline. The CEO of Honk for Hybrids, Mr. Don T. Pop, is searching for a new design team to come up with something outside the box. He wants to put a vehicle on the market that is not only cost effective but also uses alternative energy to run.

MISSION

Construct and name your balloon-powered car. The design team with the prototype that travels the farthest using only balloon power will have the opportunity to secure the contract to work for Honk for Hybrids and put their design on the market.

BLUEPRINT — EXPLORE

Provide the Individual and Group Blueprint Design Sheets to engineering teams. Have individual students sketch a prototype to present to the other members of their team. Team members will discuss the pros and cons of each sketch and then select one prototype to construct.

HONK FOR HYBRIDS

 ENGINEERING TASK **TEST TRIAL** **ANALYZE** **REDESIGN**

ENGINEERING TASK	TEST TRIAL	ANALYZE	REDESIGN
Each team will construct a balloon-powered car.	Teams will test and measure the distance (in centimeters) their balloon cars travel three times. The farthest distance will be recorded in meters. Students may blow up balloons and then tape them to the vehicle before each trial.	Facilitate analytical discussions comparing mass amounts and design features. Allow teams to reflect on their designs compared to others' and what they would do differently.	Allow teams to redesign their prototypes, including altering the original sketches using a colored pencil to show the changes they have made. The goal is a more effective car this time around.

HELPFUL TIPS

- After the Test Trial, have teams take a gallery walk to view other teams' designs for possible ideas to assist them in the Analyze and Redesign portions of the engineering design process.

- If teams are successful on the first try, encourage them to make their prototypes even more efficient. If it is a scenario in which this is not feasible, distribute team members to other teams to be a support for them in making their prototypes more efficient. Alternatively, at teacher discretion, move students on to the Justification portion of the lesson.

- If after the third test the final prototype is still unsuccessful, have students write how they would start over. These challenges are meant to have students build on what they originally designed. If the design proved to be unsuccessful, encourage a reflection or justification on what they would do if they were allowed to start again from scratch.

HONK FOR HYBRIDS

REFLECTIONS — EXPLAIN & ELABORATE

AFTER TEST TRIAL 1	Which team of engineers had the prototype that traveled the farthest? How far (in centimeters) did your balloon car travel? What were some of the differences between the prototypes?
ANALYSIS	What changes will you make so your prototype will go farther?
AFTER TEST TRIAL 2	Did the changes you made result in a more effective car? How much farther did your car travel this time (in centimeters)?
ANALYSIS	What changes did the most successful design team make to its prototype? What other changes will you make so your car prototype will go farther?
AFTER TEST TRIAL 3	Did the changes you made result in a more effective car? Which team had the most effective prototype?

JUSTIFICATION — EVALUATE

TECHNOLOGY	Record a commercial highlighting your new Honk for Hybrids balloon-powered vehicle. Upload it to the class website to share with parents and other classrooms.
ELA	A. Write a summary about the building process for the balloon-powered vehicle prototype. B. Create an informational brochure about hybrid cars. List the pros and cons of owning a hybrid car.
ARTS	Create a jingle for the balloon-powered vehicle that will be played whenever the car is advertised. Present it to the class.

STEAM Design Challenges Gr. 5 © 2017 Creative Teaching Press

ORCA OVERCAST

STEAM

3 HOURS TIME FOR COMPLETION WITH AN ADDITIONAL 2 HOURS FOR REDESIGNING AND RETESTING

DESIGN CHALLENGE PURPOSE

Design and construct a prototype of a tank for a rescued whale to reside in during her rehabilitation. It must maintain a water temperature of at or just below 80°F.

TEACHER DEVELOPMENT

Energy is the ability to do work. There are many types of energy. This lesson focuses on solar energy. **Solar energy** refers to the light energy we receive from the sun. Light and **heat** (thermal) energy are often found together. The light from the sun also transfers into heat energy, which heats our planet. Solar energy heats water, causing water temperatures to rise, which can have an adverse effect for sea animals in captivity. Providing the correct type and amount of shade over a tank can help control the water temperature and keep animals comfortable.

ORCA OVERCAST

STEAM

STUDENT DEVELOPMENT

Students will need an understanding of how light energy transfers into thermal (heat) energy. Students will need to be able to read a thermometer to collect accurate data.

Lesson Idea: Fill two cups with water. Use a thermometer to determine the temperature of the water in both cups. Record both temperatures. Place one cup outside in direct sunlight for at least one hour. Keep the other cup inside away from sunlight. After one hour, bring the first cup inside. Use a thermometer to determine the temperature of the water in both cups. Compare the new temperatures to those previously recorded.

STANDARDS

SCIENCE	TECHNOLOGY	ENGINEERING	ARTS	MATH	ELA
5-ESS3-1	ISTE.1	3-5-ETS1-1	Creating	CCSS.MATH.CONTENT.5.G.A.2	CCSS.ELA-LITERACY.W.5.2
	ISTE.4	3-5-ETS1-2	Anchor Standard #1	CCSS.MATH.PRACTICE.MP4	CCSS.ELA-LITERACY.SL.5.1.C
		3-5-ETS1-3	Anchor Standard #2		

SCIENCE & ENGINEERING PRACTICES

Obtaining, Evaluating, and Communicating Information: Obtain and combine information from books and/or other reliable media to explain phenomena or solutions to a design problem.

STEAM — ORCA OVERCAST

CROSSCUTTING CONCEPTS

Systems and System Models: A system can be described in terms of its components and their interactions.

TARGET VOCABULARY

- absorption
- energy
- heat
- insulator
- melting rate
- reflection
- solar energy

MATERIALS

- construction paper (various colors)
- aluminum foil
- wax paper
- straws
- cardboard
- tape
- thermometer
- water
- clear plastic cups

LITERACY CONNECTIONS

Energy from the Sun: Solar Power by James Bow

NOTES

ORCA OVERCAST

DILEMMA — ENGAGE

Ocean World Marine Life Rescue and Rehab Center has just found out that they will be getting a recently rescued orca whale. Unfortunately, they do not have enough room in the current tanks for their new addition! The materials used for the current tanks, such as the canopy over the tank, are no longer available, and they need to have this tank ready as soon as possible!

Dr. Larry Lobsterly, Chief Marine Biologist at Ocean World Marine Life Rescue and Rehab Center, has asked student volunteers to construct a prototype tank that will keep the sun off the rescued whale. The temperature of the water in the tank must stay at or just below 80°F so that the new whale will feel at home during its stay at the rescue and rehab center. Because the whale is coming on such short notice, there is no time to order the materials and the shade must be made using only what is currently available at the park. The group of volunteers that creates the whale tank prototype that keeps the water temperature at or just below 80°F will be part of the team that releases the rescued orca back into the wild once it is ready.

MISSION

Design and construct a whale tank prototype that will keep the temperature at or just below 80°F.

BLUEPRINT — EXPLORE

Provide the Individual and Group Blueprint Design Sheets to engineering teams. Have individual students sketch a prototype to present to the other members of their team. Team members will discuss the pros and cons of each sketch and then select one prototype to construct.

ORCA OVERCAST

 ENGINEERING TASK → **TEST TRIAL** → **ANALYZE** → **REDESIGN**

Engineering Task: Each team will construct a prototype of a whale tank.

Test Trial: Teams will test their prototypes. Ensure that they measure and record the temperature of the water every 10 minutes for 60 minutes. Remind them to record detailed observations.

Analyze: Facilitate analytical discussions comparing the design and structure of the tanks. Allow teams to reflect on their designs compared to others' and what they would do differently.

Redesign: Allow teams to redesign their prototypes, including altering the original sketches using a colored pencil to show the changes they have made. The goal is to keep the water temperature at or just below 80°F.

HELPFUL TIPS

- After the Test Trial, have teams take a gallery walk to view other teams' designs for possible ideas to assist them in the Analyze and Redesign portions of the engineering design process.

- If teams are successful on the first try, encourage them to make their prototypes even more efficient. If it is a scenario in which this is not feasible, distribute team members to other teams to be a support for them in making their prototypes more efficient. Alternatively, at teacher discretion, move students on to the Justification portion of the lesson.

- If after the third test the final prototype is still unsuccessful, have students write how they would start over. These challenges are meant to have students build on what they originally designed. If the design proved to be unsuccessful, encourage a reflection or justification on what they would do if they were allowed to start again from scratch.

ORCA OVERCAST

REFLECTIONS — EXPLAIN & ELABORATE

AFTER TEST TRIAL 1	Which team of engineers had the most effective prototype? What did other teams do that made their prototype more successful?
ANALYSIS	What changes will you make to your prototype that will keep the temperature at or just below 80°F?
AFTER TEST TRIAL 2	Did your prototype get closer to maintaining or staying just below 80°F? What changes did you make to improve your prototype?
ANALYSIS	What changes did you make to your prototype that made it more effective?
AFTER TEST TRIAL 3	If you could start over, what would you do differently to your prototype to ensure that you keep the tank at or just below 80°F?

JUSTIFICATION — EVALUATE

TECHNOLOGY	Create a presentation that includes a graph representing the data you collected. Use what you learned about light and solar energy to explain the results your prototype produced during the challenge.
ELA	Write a letter to Dr. Lobsterly to convince him to choose your prototype.
ARTS	Create a poster for Ocean World Marine Life Rescue and Rehab Center showing your prototype tank and any additional special features not included in the design challenge that might support the new whale.
MATH	Create a graph of the temperature data collected during the design challenge.

STOW FOR THE CROW

STEAM

1 HOUR TIME FOR COMPLETION

DESIGN CHALLENGE PURPOSE

Design a container that holds the greatest volume.

TEACHER DEVELOPMENT

This lesson should be used as an exploration of the **volume** or **capacity** of a container prior to teaching the concepts of volume in terms of multiplication and addition. The goal of the lesson is to have students manipulate a piece of paper to create a three-dimensional figure with the largest capacity. In order to determine the amount of material being added, students will need to measure and keep track of how much material they are placing in their figure. As students begin to analyze their structure and redesign, they will see that the typical rectangle does not necessarily produce the largest volume. Encourage students to be creative in how they manipulate the paper to create their structure. Utilizing tape for their structure is best as it allows them to adjust the placement, unlike glue and staples, which are more difficult to reposition.

STOW FOR THE CROW

STUDENT DEVELOPMENT

Students will need to understand that the concept of volume focuses on filling a three-dimensional figure.

Lesson Idea: Take a paper cup and a plastic cup that have different volumes. Ensure that the cup with the smaller volume weighs more. For example, use a styrofoam cup and a glass cup.

Show the cups to the students. Ask students to predict which cup weighs more. Many students will pick the cup that is larger in size.

Ask students to predict which cup has the greater volume. Place students into groups of four. Give each team one of each type of cup. Have the teams fill the cups with Skittles (counting as they go). Once each team has filled its cup, discuss which cup has the greater volume and why. Explain that volume has to do with how much space is inside an object.

STANDARDS

SCIENCE	TECHNOLOGY	ENGINEERING	ARTS	MATH	ELA
		3-5-ETS1-1		CCSS.MATH.CONTENT.5.MD.A.1	CCSS.ELA-LITERACY.W.5.1
		3-5-ETS1-2		CCSS.MATH.CONTENT.5.MD.C.3B	CCSS.ELA-LITERACY.SL.5.5
		3-5-ETS1-3		CCSS.MATH.CONTENT.5.MD.C.4	CCSS.ELA-LITERACY.SL.5.1.C
				CCSS.MATH.CONTENT.5.MD.C.5	

SCIENCE & ENGINEERING PRACTICES

Asking Questions and Defining Problems: Define a simple design problem that can be solved through the development of an object, tool, process, or system and includes several criteria for success and constraints on materials, time, or cost.

Planning and Carrying Out Investigations: Plan and conduct an investigation collaboratively to produce data to serve as the basis for evidence, using fair tests in which variables are controlled and the number of trials considered.

Constructing Explanations and Designing Solutions: Generate and compare multiple solutions to a problem based on how well they meet the criteria and constraints of the design problem.

STOW FOR THE CROW

CROSSCUTTING CONCEPTS

Influence of Engineering, Technology, and Science on Society and the Natural World: People's needs and wants change over time, as do their demands for new and improved technologies.

Engineers improve existing technologies or develop new ones to increase their benefits, decrease known risks, and meet societal demands.

TARGET VOCABULARY

capacity

volume

MATERIALS

- paper
- scissors
- tape
- measuring cups
- fable ("The Crow and the Pitcher" by Aesop)
- sand/dirt/rice (something to fill container)

Select one material that all students will use to fill their container.

LITERACY CONNECTIONS

The Classic Treasury of Aesop's Fables by Don Daily

NOTES

STOW FOR THE CROW

DILEMMA — ENGAGE

Read "The Crow and the Pitcher" by Aesop.

Crosby the Crow is very thirsty! He is hiring your team of engineers to create a new water container that will have the most volume. Your team will receive one piece of paper, a pair of scissors, and a roll of tape to construct a container and solve Crosby's dilemma.

MISSION

Construct a container that holds the largest possible volume but still allows Crosby the Crow to easily access what is inside.

BLUEPRINT — EXPLORE

Provide the Individual and Group Blueprint Design Sheets to engineering teams. Have individual students sketch a prototype to present to the other members of their team. Team members will discuss the pros and cons of each sketch and then select one prototype to construct.

STEAM Design Challenges Gr. 5 © 2017 Creative Teaching Press

STOW FOR THE CROW

 ENGINEERING TASK → **TEST TRIAL** → **ANALYZE** → **REDESIGN**

Engineering Task: Each team will design and construct a water container that holds the largest possible volume but still allows Crosby to easily access what is inside.

Test Trial: Teams will measure the amount of sand/dirt/rice and keep track as they test the volume of their containers. Teams should record their measurements.

Analyze: Students should have the opportunity to add their volume to a class chart. Design teams should rethink their designs and make changes on their blueprints.

Redesign: Design teams should have the opportunity to reconfigure their prototypes for a larger volume.

HELPFUL TIPS

- After the Test Trial, have teams take a gallery walk to view other teams' designs for possible ideas to assist them in the Analyze and Redesign portions of the engineering design process.

- If teams are successful on the first try, encourage them to make their prototypes even more efficient. If it is a scenario in which this is not feasible, distribute team members to other teams to be a support for them in making their prototypes more efficient. Alternatively, at teacher discretion, move students on to the Justification portion of the lesson.

- If after the third test the final prototype is still unsuccessful, have students write how they would start over. These challenges are meant to have students build on what they originally designed. If the design proved to be unsuccessful, encourage a reflection or justification on what they would do if they were allowed to start again from scratch.

STOW FOR THE CROW

REFLECTIONS — EXPLAIN & ELABORATE

AFTER TEST TRIAL 1
What is the volume of your prototype?
What unit of measurement did you use?

ANALYSIS
What observations did you make while looking at other teams' containers?
What was the difference between the largest and smallest volume?
What adjustments will you make to your prototype to increase its volume?

AFTER TEST TRIAL 2
Did your redesign increase or decrease the volume? Why?

ANALYSIS
What did you do that increased or decreased the volume?
What changes would you like to make before Trial 3?
Why are you making those changes?

AFTER TEST TRIAL 3
Did the adjustments to your prototype increase the volume?
Were there any difficulties as you changed your container for the third time? Explain.
What could your team do differently if you could build another prototype?

JUSTIFICATION — EVALUATE

ELA
Write your own fable. Make sure it has a moral.

MATH
Convert the units of measurement you used during the challenge into a smaller or larger unit.

CRITTER CREATIONS

STeAm

SETTING THE STAGE

DESIGN CHALLENGE PURPOSE

Design a new species of animal that will both flourish and help restore the balance of its designated ecosystem.

TEACHER DEVELOPMENT

The **food chain** is a transfer of energy from one organism to another. Students often have the misconception that the food chain is about who eats whom, not about the flow of energy through the food chain. The diagram below should serve as an example of how energy flows from one organism to another in a food chain. The arrows in a food chain flow in the direction the energy is going. All sources of energy in a food chain come first from the sun.

In reality, nature is not a simple chain but a **food web** consisting of many different species of plants, animals, and decomposers. The following diagram illustrates an example of a food web. Use this image to have students label the producer, consumer, predator, and prey.

Note: For each test trial, students will be presented with a scenario card that places their animal into an environment or situation that may be different from what they had in mind when designing the animal. They may discover that the animal does not have the physical traits or adaptations to survive based on the situation described on their card. Students might also discover that other design challenge teams successfully created animals that can survive and adapt to the situations on their cards.

CRITTER CREATIONS

STUDENT DEVELOPMENT

Students will need to have an understanding of food chains and food webs. They will also need to know the following terms: *predator, prey, consumer, producer, ecosystem, extinct, endangered.*

Lesson Idea: Print out pictures of various animals and plants from the same ecosystem. Pass them out to your students. Have students form their own food web(s).

STANDARDS

SCIENCE	TECHNOLOGY	ENGINEERING	ARTS	MATH	ELA
5-LS-1	ISTE.1	3-5-ETS1-1	Creating		CCSS.ELA-LITERACY.W.5.2
	ISTE.4	3-5-ETS1-2	Anchor Standard #1		CCSS.ELA-LITERACY.SL.5.1.C
		3-5-ETS1-3			

SCIENCE & ENGINEERING PRACTICES

Developing and Using Models: Use models to describe phenomena. Develop a model to describe phenomena.

Engaging in Argument from Evidence: Support an argument with evidence, data, or a model.

CRITTER CREATIONS

CROSSCUTTING CONCEPTS

Systems and System Models: A system can be described in terms of its components and their interactions.

Energy and Matter: Matter is transported into, out of, and within systems. Energy can be transferred in various ways and between objects.

TARGET VOCABULARY

carnivore
consumer
ecosystem
endangered
extinct
food chain
food web
herbivore
omnivore
predator
prey
producer
species
vegetation

MATERIALS

- situation and scenario cards (page 133)
- clay
- sculpting tools (plastic spoons and/or craft sticks)

LITERACY CONNECTIONS

Who Eats What?: Food Chains and Food Webs
by Patricia Lauber

NOTES

CRITTER CREATIONS

DILEMMA — ENGAGE

Edward Eco of Environmental Investigations recently took a trip to Tasmania to investigate the variety of animals in one of the local ecosystems. Upon his arrival, he found that the balance was completely off due to the extinction of the Tasmanian tiger, a normal predator in the food chain of that ecosystem. The rabbit population was growing at such a rapid rate that the vegetation in the area was quickly being depleted. The more he investigated, the more he realized that there was a big problem! He reported back to his CEO, Mr. Environment, that a solution needs to be discovered immediately.

Mr. Environment's top scientist, Dr. Dee N. Aegh (D.N.A.) has the tools to create an animal, but she has no idea what kind of animal to create. She needs your help! Can you design an animal that can live in the environment of Tasmania and take the place of the Tasmanian tiger on the food chain? If you can, you will save that ecosystem. If the prototype successfully meets the requirements on the situation and scenario cards, the team will name the prototype species they designed.

MISSION

Design a new species of predator that can live in the lush forest habitat of an area in Tasmania. Will your team get to name the animal?

BLUEPRINT — EXPLORE

Provide the Individual and Group Blueprint Design Sheets to engineering teams. Have individual students sketch a prototype to present to the other members of their team. Team members will discuss the pros and cons of each sketch and then select one prototype to construct.

CRITTER CREATIONS

 ENGINEERING TASK → **TEST TRIAL** → **ANALYZE** → **REDESIGN**

ENGINEERING TASK	TEST TRIAL	ANALYZE	REDESIGN
Each team will design an animal species prototype and list all of its distinguishing traits.	Teams will put their animals through a series of tests based on the details listed on the situation and scenario cards. This will determine whether each animal will flourish in the local environment as well as the effect the animal will have on the environment.	Teams will analyze the results of the situation and scenario tests to determine the likely success of their animals.	After analyzing their data, teams go back to their submitted designs and make adjustments by altering the original sketches using a colored pencil to show the changes they have made. The goal is to improve their animal prototypes for the next trial.

HELPFUL TIPS

- After the Test Trial, have teams take a gallery walk to view other teams' designs for possible ideas to assist them in the Analyze and Redesign portions of the engineering design process.

- If teams are successful on the first try, encourage them to make their prototypes even more efficient. If it is a scenario in which this is not feasible, distribute team members to other teams to be a support for them in making their prototypes more efficient. Alternatively, at teacher discretion, move students on to the Justification portion of the lesson.

- If after the third test the final prototype is still unsuccessful, have students write how they would start over. These challenges are meant to have students build on what they originally designed. If the design proved to be unsuccessful, encourage a reflection or justification on what they would do if they were allowed to start again from scratch.

CRITTER CREATIONS

REFLECTIONS — EXPLAIN & ELABORATE

AFTER TEST TRIAL 1	Were there any situations or scenarios that your new species would not be able to handle? Explain. Would your new species be able to handle the situation described on the card? What physical features would be helpful to your animal in its new environment? Explain.
ANALYSIS	What changes could you make to the design that would help your new species deal with the first situation or scenario you were given?
AFTER TEST TRIAL 2	Were there any situations or scenarios that your new species would not be able to handle? Would your new species be able to survive the situation described on the second scenario? If yes, what traits or adaptations would help your animal survive? Would any of the other teams' animals have survived? What physical traits would have helped their animals to survive?
ANALYSIS	What changes could you make to the design that would help your new species deal with the second situation or scenario you were given?
AFTER TEST TRIAL 3	Were there any scenarios or situations that your new species would not be able to handle? What additional physical traits and adaptations would be needed to help your animal survive?

JUSTIFICATION — EVALUATE

TECHNOLOGY	Create a slide show that is part of a public awareness campaign. Talk about animals that have gone extinct over the last 50 years and other animals that are listed as endangered. Introduce the newly designed animal prototype to the public, describing the animal's traits and habitat.
ELA	Research one endangered animal. Write a short research paper about the animal, and create an informational poster, brochure, or song to support the paper.
ARTS	Create a poster to go with the public awareness campaign. In addition, create a model of the animal using materials such as clay, craft sticks, and feathers. This is a great activity to enlist the collaboration of the art teacher.

HELP! I'M HUNGRY!

2 HOURS TIME FOR COMPLETION
FOR INITIAL TEST WITH ADDITIONAL TIME OVER A TWO-WEEK PERIOD

DESIGN CHALLENGE PURPOSE

Design a way to create and sustain plant growth without soil.

TEACHER DEVELOPMENT

Plants get the materials they need for growth chiefly from air and water. **Hydroponics** is described as the technology of growing plants with nutrients and water but without the use of soil.

There are several techniques for providing plants with nutrients and water through the use of hydroponic gardening.

HELP! I'M HUNGRY!

STUDENT DEVELOPMENT

This is a culminating activity. In order to know how to solve the problems presented in this challenge, students need to have a good understanding of the water cycle. They also need to know the basics of sustaining plant life: air, water, and nutrients.

Lesson Idea: Place students into groups of four. Have students draw a model of the water cycle with labels. Have teams share their water cycle diagrams to ensure that all students have a firm understanding of the water cycle.

STANDARDS

SCIENCE	TECHNOLOGY	ENGINEERING	ARTS	MATH	ELA
5-LS1-1	ISTE.1	3-5-ETS1-1	Creating	CCSS.MATH.PRACTICE.MP2	CCSS.ELA-LITERACY.RI.5.7
	ISTE.4	3-5-ETS1-2	Anchor Standard #1	CCSS.MATH.PRACTICE.MP5	
		3-5-ETS1-3			

SCIENCE & ENGINEERING PRACTICES

Engaging in Argument from Evidence: Support an argument with evidence, data, or a model.

HELP! I'M HUNGRY!

CROSSCUTTING CONCEPTS

Energy and Matter: Matter is transported into, out of, and within systems.

TARGET VOCABULARY

competition
condensation
evaporation
hydroponics
precipitation
survival
water cycle

MATERIALS

- plastic bottles
- aluminum cans (empty and open on one side)
- pebbles (to represent rocky surface)
- 1/2 cup water
- lima bean seeds (4 per team)
- duct tape
- scissors
- heat lamp

LITERACY CONNECTIONS

Ready, Set, Grow! A Kid's Guide to Gardening by Rebecca Spohn

NOTES

HELP! I'M HUNGRY!

DILEMMA — ENGAGE

Survivor Man is coming to your town! He is hosting a contest for students that challenges them to provide him with a means of surviving in the wilds of the Pebble Rock Mountains for two weeks. Students must use the contents of his backpack to help him grow a food source that might sustain him for the two weeks he is scheduled to film his show. Although he might be able to find some food in the area, he really needs your help to ensure he can at least grow some of his own. Backpack items for your use include water bottles, empty aluminum cans, lima beans, and duct tape. If you'd like, you can also use loose pebbles in your prototype design similar to what is found in the area. The student team that is most successful will have their invention displayed prominently in a display case in the front office!

MISSION

Create a prototype that will allow a plant to grow without the use of soil. Will your team have the winning prototype?

BLUEPRINT — EXPLORE

Provide the Individual and Group Blueprint Design Sheets to engineering teams. Have individual students sketch a prototype to present to the other members of their team. Team members will discuss the pros and cons of each sketch and then select one prototype to construct.

HELP! I'M HUNGRY!

 ENGINEERING TASK → **TEST TRIAL** → **ANALYZE** → **REDESIGN**

Engineering Task: Each team will construct a water cycle prototype.

Test Trial: Teams will test their prototypes to see if precipitation formed within their prototypes.

This may take up to one hour under a heat lamp.

Analyze: Facilitate a discussion about whether teams' designs were successful in creating a water cycle that could sustain plant growth.

Redesign: Was the redesigned prototype more successful? Did the variable that you changed cause a better result? If not, what variable will you change next time?

HELPFUL TIPS

- After the Test Trial, have teams take a gallery walk to view other teams' designs for possible ideas to assist them in the Analyze and Redesign portions of the engineering design process.

- If teams are successful on the first try, encourage them to make their prototypes even more efficient. If it is a scenario in which this is not feasible, distribute team members to other teams to be a support for them in making their prototypes more efficient. Alternatively, at teacher discretion, move students on to the Justification portion of the lesson.

- If after the third test the final prototype is still unsuccessful, have students write how they would start over. These challenges are meant to have students build on what they originally designed. If the design proved to be unsuccessful, encourage a reflection or justification on what they would do if they were allowed to start again from scratch.

HELP! I'M HUNGRY!

REFLECTIONS — EXPLAIN & ELABORATE

AFTER TEST TRIAL 1	2-3 days after construction of prototype: Was your team successful in creating a prototype that allowed your seed to sprout and grow?
ANALYSIS	What variable can you change to enable your seed to sprout and grow?
AFTER TEST TRIAL 2	7 days after construction of prototype: Is the prototype you created allowing plant life to grow? Measure and record the height of the plant. Did your lima bean sprout and is it growing?
ANALYSIS	What one variable do you need to change to improve the results?
AFTER TEST TRIAL 3	14 days after construction of prototype: Was your team successful in creating a prototype that allowed the lima bean seeds to sprout and grow? Measure and record the height of the plant. What other changes could you make that might further improve your prototype and sustain plant growth?

JUSTIFICATION — EVALUATE

TECHNOLOGY	Create an electronic presentation about your prototype to present to Survivor Man and his show's producers.
ELA	Write a justification to the Survivor Man Production Company to promote your prototype design. Cite any information from websites, articles, and videos used as research.
ARTS	Design a magazine advertisement promoting Survivor Man that features your prototype design.
MATH	Continue to observe and record the height of your plant and the other teams' plants. Graph the data.

INVASIVE INVADERS

2-3 HOURS
TIME FOR COMPLETION
ALLOWS FOR PRESENTATIONS AND TEAM DISCUSSIONS

DESIGN CHALLENGE PURPOSE

Devise a plan for eliminating the pesky pepper plants in Pottsville.

TEACHER DEVELOPMENT

Plants need air, water, and sunlight to survive. In addition, soil provides nutrients to plants. **Invasive plants** are usually exotic, which means that the plants come from another country or area. These plants can destroy the balance of an ecosystem as they compete with the native species for water and space.

Native plants are those that are normally found in an environment or ecosystem. They are part of the normal balance in the food chain. When an invasive plant moves into an area and thrives, the population of native plants can decrease.

INVASIVE INVADERS

STUDENT DEVELOPMENT

Organisms can only survive if their needs are met. Plants need sun, air, and water to survive. Soil provides nutrients that help plants thrive and grow. Plant reproduction is aided by birds that eat a plant's seeds and deposit them elsewhere in their waste. Students will need to understand the energy movement of birds and seeds.

Lesson Idea: Teaching food webs using birds in the examples will help students understand that seeds can be distributed to new areas by the birds eating them and then flying to new areas and excreting the seeds. Owl pellet studies are also a great experience that will help build background knowledge for students.

STANDARDS

SCIENCE	TECHNOLOGY	ENGINEERING	ARTS	MATH	ELA
5-LS2-1	ISTE.1	3-5-ETS1-1	Creating	CCSS.MATH.PRACTICE.MP2	CCSS.ELA-LITERACY.W.5.2
	ISTE.4	3-5-ETS1-2	Anchor Standard #1	CCSS.MATH.PRACTICE.MP4	CCSS.ELA-LITERACY.SL.5.1
		3-5-ETS1-3			CCSS.ELA-LITERACY.SL.5.1.A
					CCSS.ELA-LITERACY.SL.5.1.D

SCIENCE & ENGINEERING PRACTICES

Developing and Using Models: Develop a model to describe phenomena.

INVASIVE INVADERS

CROSSCUTTING CONCEPTS

Systems and System Models: A system can be described in terms of its components and their interactions.

TARGET VOCABULARY

invasive

native

seed dispersal

MATERIALS

- index cards
- access to texts or computers for research

LITERACY CONNECTIONS

Invaders
by Karen Edwards

NOTES

INVASIVE INVADERS

DILEMMA — ENGAGE

The pesky pepper plant has become a problem in the town of Pottsville! The mayor of Pottsville, Mr. Green, has noticed that the pesky pepper plant is taking over the beautiful parks, blocking the view of the beautiful pine trees that were planted to provide shade. He noticed some rare, native birds, the Kirtland's warbler, nesting in the park area over the past couple of years and wondered if maybe they had something to do with these new pesky pepper plants. He also noticed there was more bird waste throughout the park, and the local residents had been complaining about it. The mayor asked Mr. Botany at the local university to examine the waste matter of these rare bird species and report back to him as soon as possible. Mr. Botany discovered that the waste matter did contain seeds from the pesky pepper plants! Mayor Green has reached out to town residents to help find a solution. He needs to find a way to stop the birds from eating the seeds of the pesky pepper plant in order to stop the growth of more pepper plants. As a team of townspeople, your challenge is to find a way to solve this problem. Mayor Green is very specific in that the solution should only involve stopping the spread of the invasive pesky pepper plant and that no harm should come to the other living creatures, especially the endangered Kirtland's warbler. As your team of townspeople develops a plan of action, remember that the balance in an ecosystem is important to its existence and that drastic changes can cause an imbalance.

MISSION

Design a plan to get rid of the pesky pepper plant that has taken over the parks of Pottsville without harming the native pine trees or the endangered Kirtland's warblers that have started nesting in the park.

BLUEPRINT — EXPLORE

Provide the Individual and Group Blueprint Design Sheets to engineering teams. Have individual students develop a plan that would solve the problem and then present their idea to the other members of their team. Teams will discuss the pros and cons of all ideas presented and then select one plan to present to the entire class.

INVASIVE INVADERS

 ENGINEERING TASK **TEST TRIAL** **ANALYZE** **REDESIGN**

ENGINEERING TASK	TEST TRIAL	ANALYZE	REDESIGN
This activity does not require building and testing a prototype. Instead, teams will test their plans for stopping the pesky pepper plant by presenting them to their classmates. Then they will revise their plans based on feedback from classmates.	Presentation: Teams will present their plans to the class and the class will provide feedback as follows: 1. The first team presents its plan. 2. Other teams discuss that team's plan and write on an index card two things they like about the plan and one thing they think will not work. They should include the reason for their opinion or supporting evidence. 3. The teacher will collect the index cards and return them after all of the teams have presented their plans. 4. Repeat this process until all teams have presented.	Circulate and facilitate discussion as teams read and analyze their classmates' feedback.	Allow teams to redesign their plans using a colored pencil. Teams will cross out parts they want to change or add additional components to their plans.

HELPFUL TIPS

- After the Test Trial, have teams take a gallery walk to view other teams' designs for possible ideas to assist them in the Analyze and Redesign portions of the engineering design process.

- If teams are successful on the first try, encourage them to make their prototypes even more efficient. If it is a scenario in which this is not feasible, distribute team members to other teams to be a support for them in making their prototypes more efficient. Alternatively, at teacher discretion, move students on to the Justification portion of the lesson.

- If after the third test the final prototype is still unsuccessful, have students write how they would start over. These challenges are meant to have students build on what they originally designed. If the design proved to be unsuccessful, encourage a reflection or justification on what they would do if they were allowed to start again from scratch.

INVASIVE INVADERS

REFLECTIONS — EXPLAIN & ELABORATE

AFTER TEST TRIAL 1
What concerns did your classmates raise about your plan?

ANALYSIS
How can you address their concerns?
Can you add new details, change part of your plan, or supply more evidence to support existing ideas to make your plan more successful?

AFTER TEST TRIAL 2
What concerns did your classmates raise about your plan?

ANALYSIS
How can you address their concerns?
Can you add new details, change part of your plan, or supply more evidence to support existing ideas to make your plan more successful?

AFTER TEST TRIAL 3
What concerns did your classmates raise about your plan?

JUSTIFICATION — EVALUATE

ELA
Write a newspaper article about the pesky pepper plant. Describe why it is considered a pest; how it is impacting the environment; and what the mayor decided to implement (your plan) to stop the plant from spreading.

MATH
Create a line plot graph to indicate your projected rate of decline for the pesky pepper plant. You will need to create the data. Your teacher should provide a starting number for the total population count for the invasive species. The time period your graph should represent is three to six months.

PESKY PYTHONS

STeAm

10 HOURS
TIME FOR COMPLETION
SPREAD OVER SEVERAL DAYS

DESIGN CHALLENGE PURPOSE

Create a slideshow presentation containing research about pythons, an invasive species to the United States.

TEACHER DEVELOPMENT

The students will conduct research using articles and Internet resources. They will then create a slideshow presentation to represent the data they collected.

Throughout this challenge, student teams will research Everglades National Park and the resulting problems caused by the invasion of pythons.

Prior to students beginning their research, remind them about how to identify reliable resources on the web. Students should understand that many websites, including Wikipedia, are not reliable sources. However, the Fish and Wildlife Conservation website would be reliable. Remind students to document all of their resources.

PESKY PYTHONS

STUDENT DEVELOPMENT

Students must have a working knowledge of how to collect research in order to be able to create a presentation.

Students will need be able to gather data from websites and document where they got that information throughout this process.

STANDARDS

SCIENCE	TECHNOLOGY	ENGINEERING	ARTS	MATH	ELA
5-LS2-1	ISTE.3		Creating		CCSS.ELA-LITERACY.RI.5.1
	ISTE.6		Anchor Standard #1		CCSS.ELA-LITERACY.RI.5.6
			Anchor Standard #2		CCSS.ELA-LITERACY.RI.5.7
					CCSS.ELA-LITERACY.RI.5.9

SCIENCE & ENGINEERING PRACTICES

Analyzing and Interpreting Data: Analyze and interpret data to make sense of phenomena, using logical reasoning, mathematics, and/or computation.

PESKY PYTHONS

CROSSCUTTING CONCEPTS

Patterns: Similarities and differences in patterns can be used to sort, classify, communicate, and analyze simple rates of change for natural phenomena and designed products. Patterns can be used as evidence to support an explanation.

TARGET VOCABULARY

invasive

MATERIALS

- Internet
- scientific articles
- paper
- index cards for comments
- research outline (page 134)

LITERACY CONNECTIONS

Food Chain Frenzy (The Magic School Bus Chapter Book, No. 17) by Anne Capeci

What If There Were No Gray Wolves?: A Book About the Temperate Forest Ecosystem (Food Chain Reactions) by Suzanne Slade

NOTES

PESKY PYTHONS

DILEMMA — ENGAGE

Snakes Galore Inc. has noticed an increase in the number of python sightings reported across the state of Florida. Snakes Galore Inc. and its president, Mr. Slither, want to ensure the safety of the citizens in those locations and believes it is important to track the sightings of these invasive pythons to maintain the balance of the ecosystem. Mr. Slither has sent out a notice to all schools asking students to create a public awareness campaign through research and the creation of a slideshow presentation. Students will also need to determine what agency they should send their presentation to for the greatest impact.

MISSION

Research python sightings in Florida and develop a slideshow presentation with a minimum of 10 slides. Use different books, articles, and at least three websites. Include at least three diagrams or photos, slide transitions, animations, at least two geographical maps, and a bibliography. Include information about where the python originated, why it is labeled as invasive, and possible solutions to the problem. Students who meet the criteria in their presentation will be able to email it to the agency they determined would be the most impactful.

BLUEPRINT — EXPLORE

Provide the Research Outline to design teams. Teams will use the Research Outline to guide them as they gather information for their slideshow.

PESKY PYTHONS

ENGINEERING TASK	**TEST TRIAL**	**ANALYZE**	**REDESIGN**
Each team will research the python population in Florida and create a presentation.	Present the team slide show to two other teams. Those teams will give feedback on an index card. The responding teams must write two positive comments and one suggested improvement, keeping in mind the presentation requirements. The slide show must be presented to two teams before presenting it to the whole class.	Each team will review the feedback it received from the other teams who saw the presentation. Then team members will discuss what they would like to change or add to their presentation to ensure that it meets the requirements.	After discussing possible changes to their slideshow, students will write down the changes they will make to their slideshow in their notebooks or on their *Research Outline* page before making those changes to their slideshow presentation.

HELPFUL TIPS

- After the Test Trial, have teams take a gallery walk to view other teams' designs for possible ideas to assist them in the Analyze and Redesign portions of the engineering design process.

- If teams are successful on the first try, encourage them to make their prototypes even more efficient. If it is a scenario in which this is not feasible, distribute team members to other teams to be a support for them in making their prototypes more efficient. Alternatively, at teacher discretion, move students on to the Justification portion of the lesson.

- If after the third test the final prototype is still unsuccessful, have students write how they would start over. These challenges are meant to have students build on what they originally designed. If the design proved to be unsuccessful, encourage a reflection or justification on what they would do if they were allowed to start again from scratch.

PESKY PYTHONS STEAM

REFLECTIONS — EXPLAIN & ELABORATE

AFTER TEST TRIAL 1	What feedback did you receive from the first team that watched your presentation? What did they like about it? Did they notice anything missing from your presentation? What did you like about the other team's presentation? Were they missing any requirements?
ANALYSIS	What will your team add to or change in your presentation based on the feedback provided by the other team?
AFTER TEST TRIAL 2	What feedback did you receive from the second team that watched your presentation? What did they like about it? Did they notice anything missing from your presentation? What did you like about the other team's presentation? Were they missing any requirements?
ANALYSIS	What will your team add to or change in your presentation based on the feedback provided by the other team?
AFTER TEST TRIAL 3	What feedback did you receive from the whole class? What did they like about it?

JUSTIFICATION — EVALUATE

TECHNOLOGY	Research an invasive species in your area and create a slideshow presentation that includes where the invasive species originated, why it is labeled invasive, and possible solutions.
ELA	Write an informational text that explains the process of how you collected, analyzed, and displayed your research. Be sure to include interesting facts about the python as you explain the process.
ARTS	Create a "Wanted" poster to alert the public about the python problem. Include the dangers of this animal and the locations where they have been found. *Note:* Find articles in newspapers in advance of this activity to use as a resource for your students.

BLAST OFF!

STEAM

3 HOURS TIME FOR COMPLETION

SETTING THE STAGE

DESIGN CHALLENGE PURPOSE

Design and launch a rocket that travels the farthest distance, with the longest hang time, using a straw as a launch tool.

TEACHER DEVELOPMENT

Gravity is a force of attraction. Objects with mass are attracted to each other. If one object has more mass than the other, it pulls the smaller object toward it. Because our planet has so much mass, we are all pulled toward its center. That's why an object comes back down when you throw it in the air. The sun has more mass than the earth. That is why the earth orbits the sun. Earth is held in orbit by the sun's gravitational pull. **Force** is defined as a push or a pull. **Motion** is a change in the position of an object.

When force is applied to an object, it will move unless another force is preventing it from moving. Some forces, like **friction**, oppose motion. **Air resistance** is a type of friction that will affect the paper rockets in this activity. Gravity can both oppose or accelerate motion depending on the direction of the movement of an object. Forces can cause an object to accelerate (move), decelerate (slow down), or change direction.

BLAST OFF!

STUDENT DEVELOPMENT

Students will need a basic understanding of how the gravitational force of the earth acting on an object near the earth's surface pulls that object toward the planet's center. Students will also need to understand the cause and effect relationships used to explain change in direction and speed.

Note: Visit the website listed on the inside front cover to view the article suggested and help your students learn about these concepts so that they can apply their knowledge when designing their prototype for this challenge.

STANDARDS

SCIENCE	TECHNOLOGY	ENGINEERING	ARTS	MATH	ELA
5-PS2-1	ISTE.1	3-5-ETS1-1	Creating	CCSS.MATH.CONTENT.5.OA.B.3	CCSS.ELA-LITERACY.RI.5.9
		3-5-ETS1-2	Anchor Standard #1	CCSS.MATH.CONTENT.5.G.A.2	CCSS.ELA-LITERACY.SL.5.1.C
		3-5-ETS1-3	Anchor Standard #2	CCSS.MATH.PRACTICE.MP5	

SCIENCE & ENGINEERING PRACTICES

Developing and Using Models: Use models to describe phenomena.

Planning and Carrying Out Investigations: Plan and conduct an investigation collaboratively to produce data to serve as the basis for evidence, using fair tests in which variables are controlled and the number of trials considered.

Analyzing and Interpreting Data: Represent data in graphic displays (bar graphs, pictographs, and/or pie charts) to reveal patterns that indicate relationships.

Constructing Explanations and Designing Solutions: Generate and compare multiple solutions to a problem based on how well they meet the criteria and constraints of the design problem.

BLAST OFF!

CROSSCUTTING CONCEPTS

Cause and Effect: Cause and effect relationships are routinely identified and used to explain change.

Scale, Proportion, and Quantity: Natural objects exist from the very small to the immensely large.

TARGET VOCABULARY

air resistance
force
friction
gravity
hang time
height
launch
motion
structure
trajectory

MATERIALS

- straw
- meterstick/tape measure
- timer/stopwatch
- tape
- scissors
- plain white paper

LITERACY CONNECTIONS

To Fly: The Story of the Wright Brothers by Wendie C. Old

A Crash Course in Forces and Motion with Max Axiom, Super Scientist by Emily Sohn and Charles Barnett III

NOTES

BLAST OFF!

DILEMMA — ENGAGE

Build-A-Rocket has been a leader in the designing and building of Planet Martian's means of travel. With the recent change in their atmosphere and the struggle with getting materials to their facility to build these rockets, the president of the company has had to rethink how they design and build their product.

The president of Build-A-Rocket has sent out a message to neighboring planets asking for new blueprints and prototypes of a rocket using whatever materials they are able to produce on each of their planets. The winning prototype will be at least 5 in. long, travel the farthest distance, and have the longest hang time.

MISSION

Construct a rocket that will travel the farthest distance and have the longest hang time.

BLUEPRINT — EXPLORE

Provide the Individual and Group Blueprint Design Sheets to engineering teams. Have individual students sketch a prototype to present to the other members of their team. Team members will discuss the pros and cons of each sketch and then select one prototype to construct.

STEAM — BLAST OFF!

 ENGINEERING TASK **TEST TRIAL** **ANALYZE** **REDESIGN**

Engineering Task: Each team will construct a rocket prototype using the materials provided. The students will blow into the straw to launch their rockets.

Note: Launch rockets horizontally, not straight up into the air.

Test Trial: Teams will launch their prototypes three times during each test trial and measure and record both the hang time and the distance for each launch.

Note: Teams should select only one person to launch the rocket using the straw.

Analyze: Facilitate analytical discussions comparing the structure and design of the different prototypes. Allow teams to reflect on their designs compared to others and what they would do differently.

Redesign: Allow teams to redesign their prototypes, including altering the original sketches using a colored pencil to show the changes they have made. The goal is to travel a greater distance and maintain a longer hang time.

HELPFUL TIPS

- After the Test Trial, have teams take a gallery walk to view other teams' designs for possible ideas to assist them in the Analyze and Redesign portions of the engineering design process.

- If teams are successful on the first try, encourage them to make their prototypes even more efficient. If it is a scenario in which this is not feasible, distribute team members to other teams to be a support for them in making their prototypes more efficient. Alternatively, at teacher discretion, move students on to the Justification portion of the lesson.

- If after the third test the final prototype is still unsuccessful, have students write how they would start over. These challenges are meant to have students build on what they originally designed. If the design proved to be unsuccessful, encourage a reflection or justification on what they would do if they were allowed to start again from scratch.

BLAST OFF!

STEAM

REFLECTIONS — EXPLAIN & ELABORATE

AFTER TEST TRIAL 1	Which team of engineers had the most effective prototype? What were the differences between the prototypes?
ANALYSIS	Did certain design features, such as 2 vs. 3 fins, make a difference?
AFTER TEST TRIAL 2	What changes did you make to improve your prototype? How did your prototype measure up against the others?
ANALYSIS	Did your second trial have a better or worse outcome than the first? Why? What other changes would you consider in future trials?
AFTER TEST TRIAL 3	What changes did you make that helped improve your prototype? Did your prototype have the farthest distance or longest hang time? If not, why did the winning prototype win?

JUSTIFICATION — EVALUATE

TECHNOLOGY	Design a digital presentation such as a Prezi, PowerPoint, or SWAY to convince the president of Build-A-Rocket to select your prototype.
ELA	Write a justification to Build-A-Rocket explaining why your prototype should be the winning structure. Be creative! For example, write a letter, speech, or poem.
ARTS	Design an advertisement for your rocket.
MATH	Graph the data (distance and hang time) you collected in one unit of measurement. Then graph the same data again after converting to a different unit of measurement. For example, use centimeters the first time and inches the next.

STEAM Design Challenges Gr. 5 © 2017 Creative Teaching Press

EGGSTRA SAFE CARS

STEAm

3-4 HOURS
TIME FOR COMPLETION

DESIGN CHALLENGE PURPOSE

Design a car structure that will protect an egg when driven down a ramp.

TEACHER DEVELOPMENT

The purpose of this lesson is for students to design a car that will protect a raw egg as it travels down a ramp.

Earth's **gravity** pulls objects toward the center of the planet. Isaac Newton's **Laws of Motion** describe how gravity can impact objects in various ways. An object at rest will stay at rest or an object in motion will stay in motion (going the same speed and in the same direction) unless acted upon by an **unbalanced force**. An object's **acceleration** created by a force acting on the object is directly related to the amount of force (the more force, the more acceleration). For every action, there is an equal and opposite reaction.

Note: Cardboard, plywood scraps, or stiff poster board propped up on books or chairs works well to make the testing ramps.

EGGSTRA SAFE CARS

STUDENT DEVELOPMENT

Acceleration is a change in speed and direction over time. In this lesson, students will need to apply what they learned from videos and demonstrations on acceleration and Newton's laws in order to construct the prototype with the most effective speed and safety.

Lesson Idea: Place students into groups of four. Pass out a piece of masking tape, a 12-inch piece of string, and a ping-pong ball to each group. Have students tape one end of the string to the ping-pong ball and the other end of the string to the edge of a desk. Direct students to pull the ball away from and in line with the desk so the string is pulled tight and the ball is level with the other end of the string. Have students let go of the ping-pong ball (creating a pendulum motion) and observe what happens. Wait until the ball stops moving and then have students repeat the process. Have students use their knowledge of gravitational potential energy, kinetic energy, and speed to explain what they observed.

STANDARDS

SCIENCE	TECHNOLOGY	ENGINEERING	ARTS	MATH	ELA
5-PS2-1	ISTE.1	3-5-ETS1-1	Creating		CCSS.ELA-LITERACY.RI.5.4
	ISTE.4	3-5-ETS1-2	Anchor Standard #1		CCSS.ELA-LITERACY.SL.5.1.C
		3-5-ETS1-3			

SCIENCE & ENGINEERING PRACTICES

Engaging in Argument from Evidence: Support an argument with evidence, data, or a model.

EGGSTRA SAFE CARS

CROSSCUTTING CONCEPTS

Cause and Effect: Cause-and-effect relationships are routinely identified and used to explain change.

TARGET VOCABULARY

- acceleration
- capacity
- gravity
- laws of motion
- mass
- unbalanced force
- velocity

MATERIALS

- markers
- construction paper
- craft sticks
- rubber bands
- straws
- balloons
- string
- washers
- tape
- paper
- eggs
- ramp
- pennies
- scale (balance or spring)

LITERACY CONNECTIONS

Motion: Push and Pull, Fast and Slow (Amazing Science) by Darlene R. Stille

"Staying Safe in the Car and on the Bus" at http://kidshealth.org/en/kids/car-safety.html

NOTES

EGGSTRA SAFE CARS

DILEMMA — ENGAGE

Eggstra Safe Car Company has run into a problem with their latest car model, the Speed-n-Style. Customers are raving about the style of the new vehicle. However, they are not satisfied with the safety features. They demand a product that will give them both style and safety. Eggstra Safe Car Company is hiring a team of engineers to redesign the safety features in their Speed-n-Style vehicle.

MISSION

Design the safest vehicle possible for the Eggstra Safe Car Company.

BLUEPRINT — EXPLORE

Provide the Individual and Group Blueprint Design Sheets to engineering teams. Have individual students sketch a prototype to present to the other members of their team. Team members will discuss the pros and cons of each sketch and then select one prototype to construct.

EGGSTRA SAFE CARS

 ENGINEERING TASK → **TEST TRIAL** → **ANALYZE** → **REDESIGN**

Engineering Task: Each team will construct a vehicle prototype that keeps its raw egg from cracking.

Test Trial: Each team will release its vehicle down the ramp. Students will check the effectiveness of their prototype when the vehicle reaches the bottom of the ramp.

Analyze: Facilitate analytical discussions comparing design features and mass amounts. Allow teams to reflect on their designs compared to others and what they would do differently.

Redesign: Allow teams to redesign their prototypes, including altering the original sketches using a colored pencil to show the changes they have made. The goal is to design a safer vehicle this time around.

HELPFUL TIPS

- After the Test Trial, have teams take a gallery walk to view other teams' designs for possible ideas to assist them in the Analyze and Redesign portions of the engineering design process.

- If teams are successful on the first try, encourage them to make their prototypes even more efficient. If it is a scenario in which this is not feasible, distribute team members to other teams to be a support for them in making their prototypes more efficient. Alternatively, at teacher discretion, move students on to the Justification portion of the lesson.

- If after the third test the final prototype is still unsuccessful, have students write how they would start over. These challenges are meant to have students build on what they originally designed. If the design proved to be unsuccessful, encourage a reflection or justification on what they would do if they were allowed to start again from scratch.

EGGSTRA SAFE CARS

REFLECTIONS — EXPLAIN & ELABORATE

AFTER TEST TRIAL 1
Which team of engineers had the most effective prototype?
What were the differences between the safest and least safe prototype vehicles?

ANALYSIS
What changes did you make and why?
How did you use what you learned about Newton's second law of motion when making this car?
Measure the mass of your egg car including the egg. Is more or less force required to stop the car on the ramp instead of letting it free fall? Why?

AFTER TEST TRIAL 2
Which team of engineers had the most effective prototype?
What were the differences between the safest and least safe prototype vehicles?

ANALYSIS
What changes did you make and why?
How did you use what you learned about Newton's second law of motion when making this car?
Measure the mass of your car including the egg.
Is more or less force required to stop the car on the ramp instead of letting it free fall? Why?

AFTER TEST TRIAL 3
Which team of engineers had the most effective prototype?
What were the differences between the safest and least safe prototype vehicles?

JUSTIFICATION — EVALUATE

ELA/ARTS
Create an advertisement for your vehicle highlighting both the safety features and unique style. Advertisements must include graphics as well as slogans incorporating figurative language in order to hook the customer's interest.

TECHNOLOGY
Create a slideshow presentation with a proposal for your prototype. Include descriptions and purposes of your vehicle's style and safety features.

GREENHOUSE GADGETS

STEaM

1-2 HOURS FOR DESIGN AND CONSTRUCTION

TESTING WILL TAKE PLACE OVER 2 WEEKS WITH UP TO 4 WEEKS FOR REDESIGN AND RETESTING

SETTING THE STAGE

DESIGN CHALLENGE PURPOSE

Create a greenhouse that successfully grows vegetable seeds.

TEACHER DEVELOPMENT

When energy from the sun is absorbed by a plant, a chemical reaction occurs causing the formation of sugar, which serves as food for the plant. In order for this process known as **photosynthesis** to occur, plants need sunlight, water, air, and other nutrients.

The **greenhouse effect** is the trapping of the sun's heat in the lower atmosphere. This effect can be used to promote warmth for plant growth.

Lesson Idea: Read aloud the Magic School Bus book suggested in the Literacy Connections section. Pause along the way to discuss the concepts covered.

GREENHOUSE GADGETS

STUDENT DEVELOPMENT

In order to solve the problems presented in this challenge, students need to have a good understanding of the greenhouse effect. Students should also understand the process of photosynthesis and how humans get energy from both the sun and the foods they consume.

Lesson Idea: How to demonstrate the greenhouse effect. Using two identical containers, place the same amount of water in each. Take and record the temperature of the water in each container. Put one of the containers in a sealed plastic bag. Place both containers in a sunny location (or under a heat lamp to simulate the sun) for 1 hour. Take and record the temperature of each container and discuss the difference in the water temperature and what caused it.

STANDARDS

SCIENCE	TECHNOLOGY	ENGINEERING	ARTS	MATH	ELA
5-ESS3-1	ISTE.1	3-5-ETS1-1	Creating	CCSS.MATH.CONTENT.5.MD.B.2	CCSS.ELA-LITERACY.RI.5.7
	ISTE.4	3-5-ETS1-2	Anchor Standard #1	CCSS.MATH.PRACTICE.MP6	
		3-5-ETS1-3			

SCIENCE & ENGINEERING PRACTICES

Obtaining, Evaluating, and Communicating Information: Obtain and combine information from books and/or other reliable media to explain phenomena or solutions to a design problem.

GREENHOUSE GADGETS

CROSSCUTTING CONCEPTS

Systems and System Models: A system can be described in terms of its components and their interactions.

Science Addresses Questions About the Natural and Material World: Science findings are limited to questions that can be answered with empirical, or fact based, evidence.

TARGET VOCABULARY

- germinate
- greenhouse effect
- humidity
- photosynthesis

MATERIALS

- 1/3 cup of water
- 3 cups of potting soil
- aluminum foil
- compact disc cases
- empty 2 liter soda bottles
- index cards
- paper towel
- plastic freezer bags
- plastic wrap
- shoe boxes
- tape
- vegetable seeds

LITERACY CONNECTIONS

The Magic School Bus Plants Seeds: A Book About How Living Things Grow by Joanna Cole

NOTES

GREENHOUSE GADGETS

DILEMMA — ENGAGE

Your team just swam ashore after your boat sank during a storm at sea. Once on shore, you found that the island had some vegetation but no people. This is a tropical island; therefore, there is very little soil, mostly sand. In order to survive on this island until help arrives, you will need a food source. When the ship sank, several items, including vegetable seeds, washed up on shore. These items will need to be utilized in order to grow vegetables. In order to survive, you and your team will need to figure out a way to plant the seeds and get them to grow.

MISSION

Create a greenhouse prototype that supports the growth of vegetable seeds.

BLUEPRINT — EXPLORE

Provide the Individual and Group Blueprint Design Sheets to engineering teams. Have individual students sketch a prototype to present to the other members of their team. Team members will discuss the pros and cons of each sketch and then select one prototype to construct.

GREENHOUSE GADGETS

 ENGINEERING TASK → **TEST TRIAL** → **ANALYZE** → **REDESIGN**

ENGINEERING TASK	TEST TRIAL	ANALYZE	REDESIGN
Each team will construct a greenhouse prototype that will successfully grow vegetable seeds.	Teams will test their greenhouses over a two-week period, making observations and comparisons every three days. (Germination can take up to 10 days.) When students observe their seeds, they must record any seed growth to the nearest ¼ in.	Facilitate analytical discussions comparing designs and construction. Allow teams to reflect on their designs compared to others and what they would do differently.	After 10 days, allow teams to redesign their prototypes, including altering the original sketches using a colored pencil to show the changes they have made. The goal is a more effective greenhouse. The new design needs approval by all team members to move forward.

HELPFUL TIPS

- After the Test Trial, have teams take a gallery walk to view other teams' designs for possible ideas to assist them in the Analyze and Redesign portions of the engineering design process.

- If teams are successful on the first try, encourage them to make their prototypes even more efficient. If it is a scenario in which this is not feasible, distribute team members to other teams to be a support for them in making their prototypes more efficient. Alternatively, at teacher discretion, move students on to the Justification portion of the lesson.

- If after the third test the final prototype is still unsuccessful, have students write how they would start over. These challenges are meant to have students build on what they originally designed. If the design proved to be unsuccessful, encourage a reflection or justification on what they would do if they were allowed to start again from scratch.

GREENHOUSE GADGETS

REFLECTIONS — EXPLAIN & ELABORATE

AFTER TEST TRIAL 1	Which team of engineers had the most growth after the first observation? Second observation? Third observation? Did your greenhouse allow for germination of the seed?
ANALYSIS	What were the differences between the prototypes with the most and least growth of the seed?
AFTER TEST TRIAL 2	Which team of engineers had the most change in growth from the first design to the second design? What changes did you include that made your design more effective?
ANALYSIS	What were the differences between the most and least effective greenhouse prototypes?
AFTER TEST TRIAL 3	Which team of engineers had the most effective prototype? What changes did you include that made your design more effective?

JUSTIFICATION — EVALUATE

TECHNOLOGY	Create an advertisement about your prototype using Microsoft Publisher or another computer program. Be creative in your advertisement designs (e.g., include color, pictures, and lots of details.)
ELA	Write a letter to the Environmental Protection Agency convincing them to purchase your prototype design. https://www.epa.gov/students/forms/contact-us-about-environmental-education
MATH	During all observations teams were asked to measure the growth of their seed to the nearest ¼ of an inch. Now take all of your measurements and produce a line plot representing all of your data.

MAKE IT STICK

STEAM

DESIGN CHALLENGE PURPOSE

Design and test a new adhesive for the Super Space company.

TEACHER DEVELOPMENT

Matter can be found in three states, **solid**, **liquid**, and **gas**. When you combine two or more substances, you are making a **mixture**. An example for students is a snack mix containing several types of food (e.g., pretzels, bagel chips, and chocolate chips). A special kind of mixture that is so thoroughly combined that you can no longer differentiate between the individual substances or components is called a **solution**. Lemonade is a good example of a solution. The lemon juice, sugar, and water are combined so that you cannot see the individual ingredients. Mixing substances together to create a new substance does not affect the total weight of the **matter**. This can often be demonstrated through the experimentation of mixing various substances while measuring and graphing the quantities being used each time. Each time a mixture is created, there are potential changes or reactions that will occur.

MAKE IT STICK

STEAM

STUDENT DEVELOPMENT

Students must have a clear understanding of the difference between a mixture and a solution in order to complete this lesson.

Lesson Idea: Provide students with a bag of trail mix. Ask them to group like pieces together. Then make some lemonade from a powder in front of students as a demonstration, and ask them if they can separate out the powder from the water. The trail mix represents a mixture because it can be separated, while the lemonade represents a solution because you cannot easily separate its two components: water and powder.

STANDARDS

SCIENCE	TECHNOLOGY	ENGINEERING	ARTS	MATH	ELA
5-PS1-4	ISTE.1	3-5-ETS1-1	Creating	CCSS.MATH.CONTENT.5.MD.A.1	CCSS.ELA-LITERACY.W.5.2
	ISTE.4	3-5-ETS1-2	Anchor Standard #1	CCSS.MATH.PRACTICE.MP2	CCSS.ELA-LITERACY.SL.5.1.C
		3-5-ETS1-3	Anchor Standard #2	CCSS.MATH.PRACTICE.MP6	

SCIENCE & ENGINEERING PRACTICES

Developing and Using Models: Develop a model to describe phenomena.

Planning and Carrying Out Investigations: Make observations and measurements to produce data to serve as the basis for evidence for an explanation of a phenomenon.

Analyzing and Interpreting Data: Represent data in graphic displays (bar graphs, pictographs, and/or pie charts) to reveal patterns that indicate relationships.

Using Math and Computational Thinking: Describe and graph quantities such as area and volume to address scientific questions.

STEAM — MAKE IT STICK

CROSSCUTTING CONCEPTS

Cause and Effect: Cause-and-effect relationships are routinely identified and used to explain change.

Scale, Proportion, and Quantity: Natural objects exist from the very small to the immensely large.

TARGET VOCABULARY

adhesive

gas

liquid

matter

mixture

solid

solution

strength

MATERIALS

- salt
- flour
- cornstarch
- baking soda
- plastic spoon
- plastic cups
- dried beans
- index card
- water
- teaspoon measuring spoon

LITERACY CONNECTIONS

Bartholomew and the Oobleck by Dr. Seuss

NOTES

MAKE IT STICK

DILEMMA — ENGAGE

Super Space is the leading designer of gadgets that are added to each shuttle that transports people from Venus to Mars. Last month, George, the leading designer at Super Space, was stranded on Jupiter during an exploratory mission. He won't be able to return for a year! Sadly, George is the only person at Super Space who knows the secret formula for the adhesive that holds all of the gadgets in place on the shuttles. The shuttle company is ready for their next ship to be completed and has asked Super Space to be ready for a completion date of next week.

Marvin, another designer at Super Space, has called a mandatory meeting of all Super Space engineers. Marvin explained the situation to the engineers and asked for them to work in teams to develop a new adhesive that will work just like George's glue. Marvin explained that designers can only use the materials found in George's lab.

MISSION

Create an adhesive, using no more than 5 teaspoons of dry ingredients, that will adhere the highest number of beans onto an index card. The beans must remain attached to the card for 2 minutes when turned upside down.

BLUEPRINT — EXPLORE

Provide the Individual and Group Blueprint Design Sheets to engineering teams. Have individual students sketch a prototype to present to the other members of their team. Team members will discuss the pros and cons of each sketch and then select one prototype to construct.

STEAM Design Challenges Gr. 5 © 2017 Creative Teaching Press

MAKE IT STICK

 ENGINEERING TASK → **TEST TRIAL** → **ANALYZE** → **REDESIGN**

ENGINEERING TASK	TEST TRIAL	ANALYZE	REDESIGN
Teams will each measure and put no more than 5 teaspoons of dry ingredients into their cup. Then they will add 1 teaspoon of water at a time, mixing their solution, and recording the recipe.	Teams will test their glue by sticking 10 beans to an index card; allowing the glue to dry for two minutes; and turning the card upside down to see how many beans remain stuck to the card. Teams must wait the full two minutes before turning the card upside down and then time for an additional two minutes. Record detailed observations.	Students must record their results, explain what happened, and share their reasoning.	Allow teams to recreate their adhesive glue and complete the process again.

HELPFUL TIPS

- After the Test Trial, have teams take a gallery walk to view other teams' designs for possible ideas to assist them in the Analyze and Redesign portions of the engineering design process.

- If teams are successful on the first try, encourage them to make their prototypes even more efficient. If it is a scenario in which this is not feasible, distribute team members to other teams to be a support for them in making their prototypes more efficient. Alternatively, at teacher discretion, move students on to the Justification portion of the lesson.

- If after the third test the final prototype is still unsuccessful, have students write how they would start over. These challenges are meant to have students build on what they originally designed. If the design proved to be unsuccessful, encourage a reflection or justification on what they would do if they were allowed to start again from scratch.

MAKE IT STICK

STEAM

REFLECTIONS — EXPLAIN & ELABORATE

AFTER TEST TRIAL 1	What ingredients did you use to make your glue? Why? How many beans remained attached to the card?
ANALYSIS	Which team of engineers had the most effective adhesive? What are the differences between the adhesives? Did certain ingredients take more or less water to create the glue consistency you were looking for?
AFTER TEST TRIAL 2	How many more or fewer beans remained attached to the card with your new glue recipe?
ANALYSIS	What change did you make to the original adhesive recipe? Why did you make those changes? What new changes do you want to make to the recipe?
AFTER TEST TRIAL 3	How many beans remained attached to the card after the latest recipe change? If you could start over again, what would you do differently? Would you do anything the same?

JUSTIFICATION — EVALUATE

TECHNOLOGY	Create a commercial for your new adhesive using a presentation source such as OneNote or PowerPoint.
ELA	Write a justification to Marvin of Super Space explaining why your adhesive will work just as well as George's glue worked.
ARTS	Create a billboard to advertise your new adhesive.

ON TARGET

STEAm

2 HOURS
TIME FOR COMPLETION

DESIGN CHALLENGE PURPOSE

Design and construct a zip line to drop a marble precisely on a target prior to reaching the opposite end of the zip line.

TEACHER DEVELOPMENT

This design challenge is an exploration of how **gravity** acts on the earth. When students create their zip line, they will discover that if they make it too steep, they will miss their target. As the facilitator of the lesson, pose questions as teams of engineers begin to construct their zip lines. For example, *Where do you think your marble will land if you lower your starting point?* Facilitating questions will prompt students to think without providing them the answer. During this lesson students will need to understand that the placement of the weight in the cup can have an effect on how fast the cup moves and if the marble will be able to drop onto the target.

Note: This challenge requires a lot of trial and error. The first hurdle will be to determine the right angle for the zip line in order for the "bucket" to travel. After teams have determined an appropriate angle, they can focus on how to get the marble to drop onto the target. This is where they will work to find those "tricks," such as making a bump in the line to encourage the release of the cargo. This challenge requires space. The best location includes an area that has a high surface and space for the zip line to descend. For example, the top of a bookshelf down to a chair or the floor at the angle the students determine to be the best for dropping the load onto the target.

ON TARGET

STUDENT DEVELOPMENT

In order to complete this challenge, students must have an understanding of how gravity acts upon an object. Students should understand that gravity pulls an object downward toward the center of the earth. Students must understand that the more mass an object has, the more force is needed to move that object.

They will need to increase or decrease the angle of their zip line in order to accurately drop their marble on the target before it reaches the end of the line. Prior to completing the challenge, students should research to better understand zip lines and why a firefighter might use one.

STANDARDS

SCIENCE	TECHNOLOGY	ENGINEERING	ARTS	MATH	ELA
5-PS2-1	ISTE.1	3-5-ETS1-1	Creating		CCSS.ELA-LITERACY.W.5.2
	ISTE.4	3-5-ETS1-2	Anchor Standard #1		CCSS.ELA-LITERACY.SL.5.1.C
		3-5-ETS1-3			

SCIENCE & ENGINEERING PRACTICES

Developing and Using Models: Use models to describe phenomena.

Planning and Carrying Out Investigations: Plan and conduct an investigation collaboratively to produce data to serve as the basis for evidence, using fair tests in which variables are controlled and the number of trials considered.

Constructing Explanations and Designing Solutions: Generate and compare multiple solutions to a problem based on how well they meet the criteria and constraints of the design problems.

ON TARGET

CROSSCUTTING CONCEPTS

Cause and Effect: Cause-and-effect relationships are routinely identified and used to explain change.

TARGET VOCABULARY

gravity
precise
trajectory

MATERIALS

- 9 ft. of fishing line
- 1 index card
- 1 marble
- masking tape
- paper clips
- scissors
- 9" x 12" construction paper
- 1 paper cup
- colored pencils

LITERACY CONNECTIONS

Fighting Fire!: Ten of the Deadliest Fires in American History and How We Fought Them by Michael L. Cooper

NOTES

ON TARGET

DILEMMA — ENGAGE

Fred the future firefighter is enrolled at Fire University's Firefighter Academy. He has one last tactics and strategy zip line test to pass before he can become an official firefighter. Fred is usually prepared for every test. Unfortunately, he lost his planner, which contained the strategies needed to prepare for his last test. Without his planner, he doesn't know the proper angles needed to attach his zip line to each tree. On top of that, he has no time to practice releasing his equipment onto the target.

MISSION

Create a zip line that will release Fred's gear (represented by the marble) onto the target before the gear reaches the opposite end of the zip line. The prototype that releases the marble onto the target with the greatest accuracy will be used for Fred's test.

BLUEPRINT — EXPLORE

Provide the Individual and Group Blueprint Design Sheets to engineering teams. Have individual students sketch a prototype to present to the other members of their team. Team members will discuss the pros and cons of each sketch and then select one prototype to construct.

STEAm — ON TARGET

 ENGINEERING TASK → **TEST TRIAL** → **ANALYZE** → **REDESIGN**

ENGINEERING TASK	TEST TRIAL	ANALYZE	REDESIGN
Each team will construct a zip line.	Teams will test their prototypes and record their observations. Students should measure and record the distance from their target to the point where their marble landed.	Teams will analyze the results of the test and determine the causes of what they observed.	After analyzing their data, teams redesign their prototypes, including altering the original sketches using a colored pencil to show the changes they have made. The goal is to improve the accuracy of their prototypes. The new design needs approval by all team members to move forward.

HELPFUL TIPS

- After the Test Trial, have teams take a gallery walk to view other teams' designs for possible ideas to assist them in the Analyze and Redesign portions of the engineering design process.

- If teams are successful on the first try, encourage them to make their prototypes even more efficient. If it is a scenario in which this is not feasible, distribute team members to other teams to be a support for them in making their prototypes more efficient. Alternatively, at teacher discretion, move students on to the Justification portion of the lesson.

- If after the third test the final prototype is still unsuccessful, have students write how they would start over. These challenges are meant to have students build on what they originally designed. If the design proved to be unsuccessful, encourage a reflection or justification on what they would do if they were allowed to start again from scratch.

ON TARGET

REFLECTIONS — EXPLAIN & ELABORATE

AFTER TEST TRIAL 1	What were the results of your first test? Were there any teams that successfully released the gear onto the target? What differences or similarities do you see in the designs of the different team prototypes?
ANALYSIS	What changes could you make to your design that would help your prototype be more successful?
AFTER TEST TRIAL 2	What were the results of your second test? Were there any teams that successfully released the gear onto the target? What differences or similarities do you see in the designs of the different team prototypes?
ANALYSIS	What changes could you make to your design that would help your prototype be more successful?
AFTER TEST TRIAL 3	Which team of engineers had the most effective prototype? What were the differences between the prototypes? Did certain design features, such as how and where the marble was released, make a difference?

JUSTIFICATION — EVALUATE

TECHNOLOGY	Create a slideshow presentation to promote your product. Include a comparison of your results and the results of the other teams.
ELA	Write a letter to convince Fred to choose your prototype.
ARTS	Create a poster to honor firefighters, police, and other public servants who are heroes in their communities.

WACKY WATER SLIDES

3-4 HOURS
TIME FOR COMPLETION

DESIGN CHALLENGE PURPOSE

Design a water slide.

TEACHER DEVELOPMENT

Angles are geometric figures that are formed wherever two rays share a common endpoint. Angles measuring 90 degrees are labeled **right angles**. Angles measuring less than 90 degrees are labeled **acute angles**. Angles measuring greater than 90 degrees are labeled **obtuse angles**.

Sir Isaac Newton formulated the concept of inertia. **Inertia** is the law of physics that says that any object in motion will stay in motion until acted on by an equal but opposite force.

WACKY WATER SLIDES

STUDENT DEVELOPMENT

Students should review the fourth grade math standards associated with angles and their measurements. They will need to know about different types of angles and how to measure them in order to effectively complete this challenge.

Lesson Idea: Have students go on a scavenger hunt looking for angles in the classroom. Have them identify and measure at least two of each type of angle (e.g., acute, right, and obtuse) using a protractor.

STANDARDS

SCIENCE	TECHNOLOGY	ENGINEERING	ARTS	MATH	ELA
5-PS2-1	ISTE.1	3-5-ETS1-1	Creating	CCSS.MATH.CONTENT.4.G.A.1	CCSS.ELA-LITERACY.RI.5.9
	ISTE.4	3-5-ETS1-2	Anchor Standard #1		
		3-5-ETS1-3			

SCIENCE & ENGINEERING PRACTICES

Engaging in Argument from Evidence: Support an argument with evidence, data, or a model.

WACKY WATER SLIDES

CROSSCUTTING CONCEPTS

Cause and Effect: Cause-and-effect relationships are routinely identified and used to explain change.

TARGET VOCABULARY

acute angle

inertia

obtuse angle

right angle

MATERIALS

- ¼ stick modeling clay
- 1 small paper cup
- Q-tips
- drinking straws
- 20 index cards
- marble
- masking tape (12 in.)
- measuring tape
- scissors
- protractor
- rubric (page 135)

LITERACY CONNECTIONS

Shape Up! Fun With Triangles and Other Polygons by David A. Adler

The Greedy Triangle by Marilyn Burns and Gordon Silveria

NOTES

WACKY WATER SLIDES

DILEMMA — ENGAGE

XYZ Water Parks is a company that builds and operates large water parks near U.S. rivers. These parks are popular for their elaborate, but safe, water slides. XYZ Water Parks will be building a new park and has chosen your city for its new location. The new water slide will attract people from miles around. The owners of XYZ Water Parks are holding a design contest. Participants will build a water slide prototype. They will be allowed five marble rolls during each of the three test trials. All marbles will be released from the top of the slide.

Prototypes will be rated by a special point system. Designs will receive points for meeting the following criteria:

- 1 point for each centimeter of height (at the highest point)
- 2 points for each marble that travels the entire length of the slide
- 5 points for each 90° angle turn in the track
- 2 points for each marble that lands in the cup

The team with the most points will have the winning design.

MISSION

Design, build, and name your water slide. The team with the winning prototype will have the water park named after them.

BLUEPRINT — EXPLORE

Provide the Individual and Group Blueprint Design Sheets to engineering teams. Have individual students sketch a prototype to present to the other members of their team. Team members will discuss the pros and cons of each sketch and then select one prototype to construct.

STEAM — WACKY WATER SLIDES

 ENGINEERING TASK → **TEST TRIAL** → **ANALYZE** → **REDESIGN**

ENGINEERING TASK	TEST TRIAL	ANALYZE	REDESIGN
Each team will construct a water slide by creating a freestanding structure that will have a track on which a marble can travel and land in a paper cup.	Teams will test their water slides five times during each test trial.	Facilitate analytical discussions comparing design features. Allow team members to reflect on their design compared to others and what they would do differently.	Allow teams to redesign their prototypes, including altering the original sketches using a colored pencil to show the changes they have made. The goal is to design a more effective water slide this time around.

HELPFUL TIPS

- After the Test Trial, have teams take a gallery walk to view other teams' designs for possible ideas to assist them in the Analyze and Redesign portions of the engineering design process.

- If teams are successful on the first try, encourage them to make their prototypes even more efficient. If it is a scenario in which this is not feasible, distribute team members to other teams to be a support for them in making their prototypes more efficient. Alternatively, at teacher discretion, move students on to the Justification portion of the lesson.

- If after the third test the final prototype is still unsuccessful, have students write how they would start over. These challenges are meant to have students build on what they originally designed. If the design proved to be unsuccessful, encourage a reflection or justification on what they would do if they were allowed to start again from scratch.

WACKY WATER SLIDES

REFLECTIONS — EXPLAIN & ELABORATE

AFTER TEST TRIAL 1	Which team of engineers had the most effective prototype? How many trials did the marble land in the cup?
ANALYSIS	Was your slide successful or in need of alteration? Why? What changes can you make to your prototype to ensure that the marble goes into the cup consistently?
AFTER TEST TRIAL 2	Which team of engineers increased their points? What changes did you include that allowed your team to earn more points?
ANALYSIS	What alterations made your prototype more successful? Could your team make further alterations to increase the number of points earned after two trials?
AFTER TEST TRIAL 3	What alterations made your prototype more successful? Could your team make further alterations to increase the number of points earned after three trials?

JUSTIFICATION — EVALUATE

TECHNOLOGY	Use a computer program to create an advertisement for your prototype. Be creative in your advertisement designs. Include color, pictures, and descriptive words.
ELA	Write a persuasive letter to XYZ Water Parks convincing the company to purchase your design.

APPENDIX

Lesson Plan-Specific Reproducibles 129

Individual Blueprint Design Sheet 136

Group Blueprint Design Sheet 137

Graph 138

Budget Planning Chart 139

STEAM Job Cards 140

Science Notebook Cover 141

STEAM Money 142

STEAM Rubric 144

Glossary 146

Bibliography 151

I CAN SEE CLEARLY NOW - EYE CHART

EYE CHART	
1	CANUSEEMEE
2	22ICKY4MEUCAN
3	HOWABOUTNOWNO
4	ALMOSTPERFECTUTHINK
5	CANYOUSEECLEARLYNOWME2

EYE CHART	
1	CANUSEEMEE
2	22ICKY4MEUCAN
3	HOWABOUTNOWNO
4	ALMOSTPERFECTUTHINK
5	CANYOUSEECLEARLYNOWME2

EYE CHART	
1	CANUSEEMEE
2	22ICKY4MEUCAN
3	HOWABOUTNOWNO
4	ALMOSTPERFECTUTHINK
5	CANYOUSEECLEARLYNOWME2

EYE CHART	
1	CANUSEEMEE
2	22ICKY4MEUCAN
3	HOWABOUTNOWNO
4	ALMOSTPERFECTUTHINK
5	CANYOUSEECLEARLYNOWME2

I CAN SEE CLEARLY NOW - RUBRIC

RATING	RUBRIC CRITERIA FOR RATING
3	**Success!!!** You can clearly see all the letters in the fifth row.
2	**Modify it!** You can make out most of the letters in the fifth row but not all. You can not see them clearly.
1	**Overhaul in your redesign...** You can make out most of the letters in the fifth row but not all six. You can not see them clearly.

RATING	RUBRIC CRITERIA FOR RATING
3	**Success!!!** You can clearly see all the letters in the fifth row.
2	**Modify it!** You can make out most of the letters in the fifth row but not all. You can not see them clearly.
1	**Overhaul in your redesign...** You can make out most of the letters in the fifth row but not all six. You can not see them clearly.

RATING	RUBRIC CRITERIA FOR RATING
3	**Success!!!** You can clearly see all the letters in the fifth row.
2	**Modify it!** You can make out most of the letters in the fifth row but not all. You can not see them clearly.
1	**Overhaul in your redesign...** You can make out most of the letters in the fifth row but not all six. You can not see them clearly.

RATING	RUBRIC CRITERIA FOR RATING
3	**Success!!!** You can clearly see all the letters in the fifth row.
2	**Modify it!** You can make out most of the letters in the fifth row but not all. You can not see them clearly.
1	**Overhaul in your redesign...** You can make out most of the letters in the fifth row but not all six. You can not see them clearly.

I CAN SEE CLEARLY NOW – STOCK CERTIFICATE

BUILD A BETTER BRIDGE - PERMIT

PERMIT

BRIDGEVILLE BUILDING DEPARTMENT

BRIDGEVILLE BUILDING DEPT. — APPROVED

DESCRIPTION OF WORK:

_____

_____

_____

_____

ISSUED: _____

EXPIRES: _____

_____
CHIEF CIVIL ENGINEER

_____
COMMISSIONER OF BUILDINGS

CRITTER CREATIONS - SITUATION AND SCENARIO CARDS

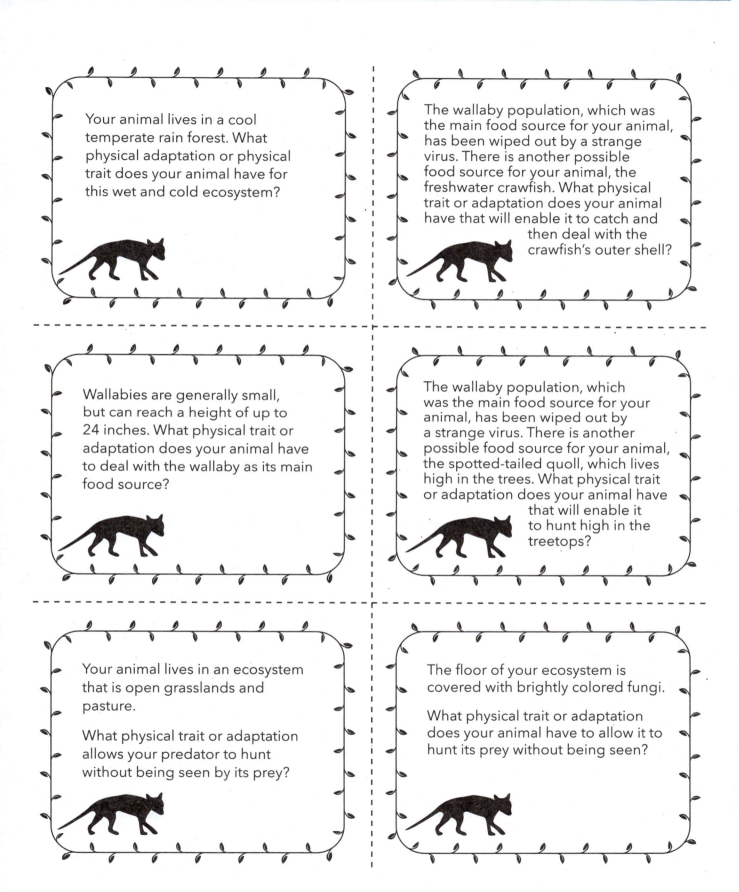

Your animal lives in a cool temperate rain forest. What physical adaptation or physical trait does your animal have for this wet and cold ecosystem?

The wallaby population, which was the main food source for your animal, has been wiped out by a strange virus. There is another possible food source for your animal, the freshwater crawfish. What physical trait or adaptation does your animal have that will enable it to catch and then deal with the crawfish's outer shell?

Wallabies are generally small, but can reach a height of up to 24 inches. What physical trait or adaptation does your animal have to deal with the wallaby as its main food source?

The wallaby population, which was the main food source for your animal, has been wiped out by a strange virus. There is another possible food source for your animal, the spotted-tailed quoll, which lives high in the trees. What physical trait or adaptation does your animal have that will enable it to hunt high in the treetops?

Your animal lives in an ecosystem that is open grasslands and pasture.

What physical trait or adaptation allows your predator to hunt without being seen by its prey?

The floor of your ecosystem is covered with brightly colored fungi.

What physical trait or adaptation does your animal have to allow it to hunt its prey without being seen?

PESKY PYTHONS - RESEARCH OUTLINE

Website: _____

Three Details:
- _____
- _____
- _____

Summary: _____
_____
_____

Website: _____

Three Details:
- _____
- _____
- _____

Summary: _____
_____
_____

Website: _____

Three Details:
- _____
- _____
- _____

Summary: _____
_____
_____

WACKY WATERSLIDES - RUBRIC

POINT RUBRIC

	Trial 1	Trial 2	Trial 3	Trial 4	Trial 5	Total
height in centimeters 1 cm = 1 point						
marble travels entire length of slide 2 points for each completion						
90° angle in the track 5 points for each 90° angle						
marble lands in the cup 2 points						

Grand Total: _____

POINT RUBRIC

	Trial 1	Trial 2	Trial 3	Trial 4	Trial 5	Total
height in centimeters 1 cm = 1 point						
marble travels entire length of slide 2 points for each completion						
90° angle in the track 5 points for each 90° angle						
marble lands in the cup 2 points						

Grand Total: _____

POINT RUBRIC

	Trial 1	Trial 2	Trial 3	Trial 4	Trial 5	Total
height in centimeters 1 cm = 1 point						
marble travels entire length of slide 2 points for each completion						
90° angle in the track 5 points for each 90° angle						
marble lands in the cup 2 points						

Grand Total: _____

POINT RUBRIC

	Trial 1	Trial 2	Trial 3	Trial 4	Trial 5	Total
height in centimeters 1 cm = 1 point						
marble travels entire length of slide 2 points for each completion						
90° angle in the track 5 points for each 90° angle						
marble lands in the cup 2 points						

Grand Total: _____

STEAM Design Challenges Gr. 5 © 2017 Creative Teaching Press

INDIVIDUAL BLUEPRINT DESIGN SHEET

TEAM MEMBER NAMES	PROS OF DESIGN	CONS OF DESIGN

GROUP BLUEPRINT DESIGN SHEET

TEAM REASONING

TEACHER APPROVAL:

GRAPH

TITLE:

BUDGET PLANNING CHART

TITLE:

MATERIALS	COST	1st TEST TRIAL		2nd TEST TRIAL		3rd TEST TRIAL	
		ITEM(S)	AMOUNT	ITEM(S)	AMOUNT	ITEM(S)	AMOUNT
TOTAL COST:							

STEAM JOB CARDS

Assigning students roles, or jobs, often helps them to collaborate by giving them some guidelines to follow. As they become more practiced at problem solving, communicating, and collaborating, they will fall into these roles naturally. In the meantime, we've provided these cards, which describe each job on their collaborative team.

Construction Specialist

Description: This person is the one whose design was chosen. This person builds the prototype and is responsible for ensuring that the prototype follows the design parameters exactly.

Material Resource Officer

Description: This person is in charge of measuring, cutting, and procuring materials for the prototype. This person assists the construction specialist by getting materials ready and assisting in construction.

Engineering Supervisor

Description: This person is the team leader. This person assists all other team members as needed. This person acts as spokesperson for the team. This person will test the team's prototype.

Administrative Contractor

Description: This person is responsible for overseeing the construction specialist. This person must measure or otherwise ensure that prototype construction matches the blueprint design.

(Use only with groups of five.)

Accounts Manager

Description: This person holds the purse strings, keeps the team's finance records (budget sheet), and pays for all materials. This person assists the engineering supervisor with testing and recording all data.

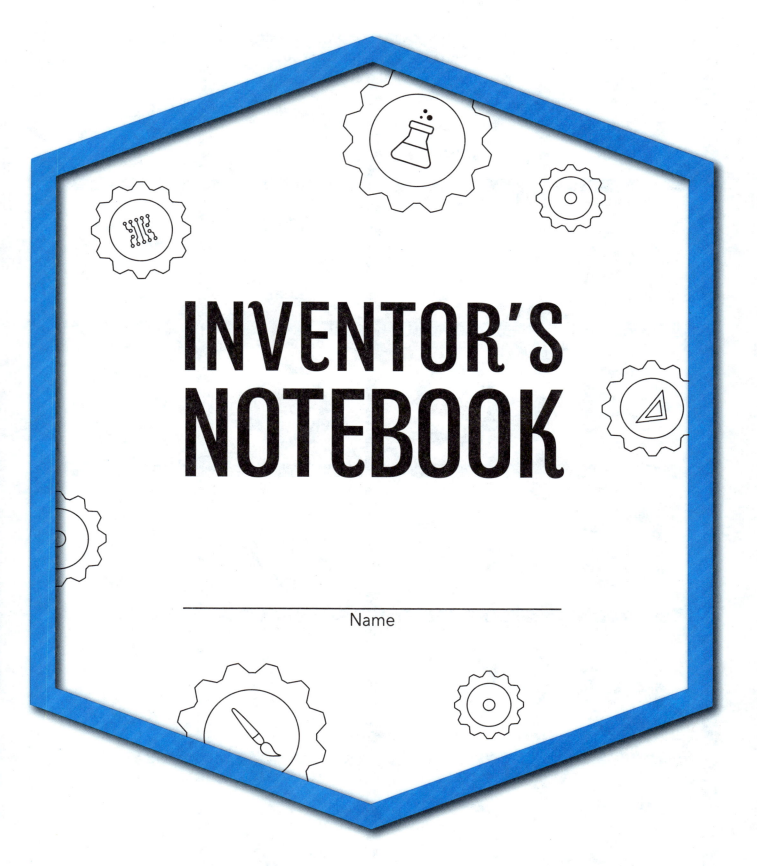

STEAM MONEY

ONE DOLLAR
$1
ONE DOLLAR
$1
ONE DOLLAR
$1
ONE DOLLAR
$1
ONE DOLLAR
$1
ONE DOLLAR
$1
ONE DOLLAR
$1
ONE DOLLAR
$1
ONE DOLLAR
$1
ONE DOLLAR
$1
ONE DOLLAR
$1
ONE DOLLAR
$1
FIVE DOLLARS
$5
FIVE DOLLARS
$5
FIVE DOLLARS
$5
FIVE DOLLARS
$5
FIVE DOLLARS
$5
FIVE DOLLARS
$5
FIVE DOLLARS
$5
FIVE DOLLARS
$5
FIVE DOLLARS
$5
FIVE DOLLARS
$5
FIVE DOLLARS
$5
FIVE DOLLARS
$5

STEAM MONEY

STEAM DESIGN CHALLENGES TEAM RUBRIC

	EXEMPLARY	PROFICIENT	PROGRESSING	BEGINNING
DESIGN	Team members reach consensus as to which prototype to construct. They complete team blueprint design sheet in which they include their reasons for selecting the team prototype. They include a written explanation to compare and contrast the prototypes they sketched individually. Prototype is constructed according to specifications in the team blueprint design.	Team members reach consensus as to which prototype to construct. They include their reasons for selecting the prototype but do not include a written explanation to compare and contrast the prototypes they sketched individually. Prototype is constructed according to the specifications in the team blueprint design.	Team members reach consensus as to which prototype to construct. They include their reasons for selecting the prototype but do not include a written explanation to compare and contrast the prototypes they sketched individually. Prototype is not constructed according to the specifications of the blueprint design.	Team members reach consensus as to which prototype to construct. They do not include either their reasons for selecting the prototype or a written explanation to compare and contrast the prototypes they sketched. Prototype is constructed.
TEST	Teams test their prototype. They record observations that align with the design challenge. They make note of any unique design flaws.	Teams test their prototype and record observations that align with the design challenge.	Teams test their prototype. They record observations that do not align with the design challenge.	Teams test their prototype. They do not record observations.

STEAM DESIGN CHALLENGES TEAM RUBRIC

	EXEMPLARY	PROFICIENT	PROGRESSING	BEGINNING
ANALYZE	Team members participate in an analytic discussion about their testing and observations. They reflect on their design as compared to at least three other teams. They discuss their intended redesign steps, defending their reasoning in their discussion.	Team members participate in an analytic discussion about their testing and observations. They reflect on their design as compared to at least two other teams. They discuss their intended redesign steps.	Team members participate in an analytic discussion about their testing and observations, comparing their design with at least one other team's. They discuss their intended redesign steps.	Team members participate in an analytic discussion about their testing but do not compare their design with another team's. They discuss their intended redesign steps.
REDESIGN	Team redesigns its prototype. Original sketch is altered using a colored pencil to illustrate changes made with supporting reasons.	Team redesigns its prototype. Original sketch is altered using a colored pencil to illustrate changes made.	Team redesigns its prototype. Original sketch is altered to illustrate changes made.	Team redesigns its prototype.
EVALUATE	Team completes a justification activity. Team reflects and makes meaningful connections to the science standards as well as to two of the other STEAM standards addressed in the lesson.	Team completes a justification activity. Team reflects and makes meaningful connections to the science standards as well as to one of the other STEAM standards addressed in the lesson.	Team completes a justification activity. Team reflects and makes meaningful connections to the science standards addressed in the lesson.	Team completes a justification activity. Team makes no connection to the science standards addressed in the lesson.

GLOSSARY

WORD	DEFINITION
absorption	The process of taking in and holding.
acceleration	A speeding up.
accurate	Free of mistakes or errors.
acute angle	An angle measuring less than 90 degrees.
adhesive	Tending to stick; a sticky substance.
air resistance	A type of friction acting opposite to the motion of another object moving through the air.
aquifer	A layer of rock or sand that can absorb and hold water.
Arctic	Relating to the North Pole or to the region around it; very cold.
atmosphere	The layers of air that surround Earth's surface.
balanced force	Two forces of equal magnitude acting in opposite directions on an object.
biosphere	The part of the earth in which life can exist.
blueprint	A detailed plan of something to be done.
capacity	The ability to contain something; the volume of a container.
carnivore	An animal that eats only other animals.
clarity	The state of being clear.
competition	When two or more organisms compete for the same resources.
condensation	The change of state from a gas to a liquid.
consumer	An organism that eats other living things to get energy.
drought	Lack of rain or water in a certain area over a long period of time.

WORD	DEFINITION
ecosystem	All living and nonliving things that exist and interact in one place.
energy	The ability to cause change or do work.
endangered	A species as risk for extinction.
engineer	To plan or build. A person who specializes in engineering.
evaporation	The change of state from a liquid to a gas.
extinct	No longer living. When the last member of a species has died, the species is extinct.
food chain	The path that food energy takes in an ecosystem as one living thing eats another.
food web	Two or more food chains that overlap.
force	A push or pull that changes the speed or direction of an object's motion.
freshwater	Water that is not salty.
friction	The rubbing of one thing against another; resistance to motion between objects in contact.
gas	A state of matter that has no definite shape and that expands to fill the container it is in.
geosphere	The solid part of Earth that includes all of the rocks and minerals on or below Earth's surface.
germinate	The process in which a seed begins to grow into a plant.
gnomon	The pin of a sundial.
gravity	The force that pulls objects or bodies toward other objects or bodies.
greenhouse effect	The process during which heat from the sun builds up near Earth's surface and is trapped there by the atmosphere.
hang time	The amount of time that something (especially a ball that is hit, kicked, or thrown) stays in the air.
heat	The measure of how much thermal energy is transferred from one thing to another.
height	The distance from the bottom to the top of something standing upright.
herbivore	An animal that eats only plants.
humidity	The degree of wetness or moisture in the air.

WORD	DEFINITION
hydroponics	A method of growing plants in water rather than in soil.
hydroponics	A method of growing plants in water rather than in soil.
inertia	(See first law of motion.)
insulator	A material that prevents electricity from flowing through it easily.
invasive	Tending to spread, often in an undesirable way.
launch	To throw or send off, especially with force; to give a start to.
laws of motion	Three laws developed by Sir Isaac Newton that outline the ways motion can be explained. • First Law—An object at rest will stay at rest or an object in motion will stay in motion (going in the same direction and at the same speed) unless acted upon by an unbalanced force. • Second Law—An object's acceleration created by a force acting on the object is directly related to the amount of force (the more force, the more acceleration) • Third Law—For every action, there is an equal and opposite reaction.
liquid	A state of matter that is neither solid nor gas.
lithosphere	The outer part of the earth consisting of the upper mantle and the crust
load	A mass or weight supported by something.
mass	The amount of matter in an object.
matter	Anything that has mass and takes up space.
melting rate	The rate at which a solid changes into a liquid through the use of heat.
mixture	Two or more substances mixed together in such a way that each remains unchanged.
motion	The act of changing place or position.
native	Born in or originate from a certain place.
natural resource	A material found in nature that is useful to people.
obtuse angle	An angle measuring greater than 90 degrees.

WORD	DEFINITION
omnivore	An animal that eats both plants and animals.
photosynthesis	The process plants use to make food.
pollution	The addition of harmful materials to the air, water, or soil.
precipitation	A form of water that falls from the clouds onto Earth's surface.
precise	Very accurate and exact.
predator	An animal that hunts other animals for food.
prey	An animal hunted or killed by another animal for food.
producer	Any organism that makes its own food.
rain barrel	A storage tank that collects rainwater.
reflection	What happens when light waves bounce off a surface.
reservoir	A place where something (like water) is kept for future use.
right angle	An angle measuring 90 degrees.
seed dispersal	The scattering or carrying away of seeds from the plant that produced them.
shadow	The dark figure cast on a surface by an object that is between the surface and the light.
shelter	Something that covers or protects; a place of safety.
solar energy	Energy emitted by the sun.
solid	A state of matter that keeps its size and shape.
solution	A liquid in which something has been dissolved.
span	The spread or distance from one support to another.
species	A group of organisms that produce organisms of the same kind.
speed	The measurement of the distance an object travels in a certain amount of time.
strength	Power to resist force.

WORD	DEFINITION
structure	The arrangement or relationship of parts.
sundial	A device to show the time of day by the position of the shadow cast onto a marked plate by an object with a straight edge.
survive	To continue to live.
temperature	A measure of how hot or cold something is.
trajectory	The curved path along which something (such as a rocket) moves through the air or through space.
unbalanced force	Forces of unequal magnitude acting on an object to create acceleration.
vegetation	Plant life.
velocity	A measure of speed in a certain direction.
volume	The amount of space that matter takes up.
water cycle	The movement of water into the air as water vapor and back to Earth's surface as precipitation.
water demand	The measure of the total amount of water used by people within the water system.
water quality	The measure of the condition of water based on the amount of pollutants found in the water

BIBLIOGRAPHY

"5th Grade Measurement and Data." K-5 Math Teaching Resources. Accessed July 18, 2016. http://www.k-5mathteachingresources.com/5th-grade-measurement-and-data.html.

Boothroyd, Jennifer. *Give It a Push! Give It a Pull!: A Look at Forces*. Minneapolis: Lerner Publishing Group, 2010.

"Cubes." *Illuminations*. National Council of Teachers of Mathematics. Accessed July 16, 2016. https://illuminations.nctm.org/Activity.aspx?id=4095.

"Drought for Kids." National Drought Mitigation Center. Accessed July 16, 2016. http://drought.unl.edu/droughtforkids.aspx.

Free Fall and Air Resistance. The Physics Classroom. Accessed July 12, 2016. http://www.physicsclassroom.com/class/newtlaws/Lesson-3/Free-Fall-and-Air-Resistance

"Gateway to invasive species information; covering Federal, State, local, and international sources." National Invasive Species Information Center. Accessed May 25, 2016. https://www.invasivespeciesinfo.gov/index.shtml.

Hall, Nancy, ed. "Newton's Laws of Motion." NASA Glenn Research Center. Accessed April 12, 2016. https://www.grc.nasa.gov/www/k-12/airplane/newton.html.

Hill, Jacob. "Invasive Species: How They Affect the Environment." EnvironmentalScience.org. Accessed July 2016. http://www.environmentalscience.org/invasive-species.

"Inertia." Merriam-Webster.com. Accessed July 8, 2016. http://www.merriam-webster.com/dictionary/inertia.

"Intermediate Energy Infobook." The NEED Project. Accessed May 2016. http://www.need.org/files/curriculum/infobook/SolarI.pdf.

Kraus, Stephanie. "Pythons Attack the Everglades." Time for Kids. Accessed July 2016. http://www.timeforkids.com/news/pythons-attack-everglades/28101.

Marie, Niclas. "When Time Began: The History and Science of Sundials." TimeCenter. Accessed June 8, 2016. https://www.timecenter.com/articles/when-time-began-the-history-and-science-of-sundials/.

"Mixtures." Study Jams. Accessed July 20, 2016. http://studyjams.scholastic.com/studyjams/jams/science/matter/mixtures.htm.

Morse, Elizabeth, and Andrew Turgeon. "Solar Energy." National Geographic Online Encyclopedia. Accessed July 25, 2016. http://nationalgeographic.org/encyclopedia/solar-energy/.

Murray, Michael. "Angle Information." Oswego City School District Regents Exam Prep Center. Accessed July 1, 2016. http://www.regentsprep.org/regents/math/geometry/gp5/langles.htm.

Perlman, Howard. "Summary of the Water Cycle." USGS Water Science School. Accessed July 10, 2016. http://water.usgs.gov/edu/watercyclesummary.html.

Perlman, Howard. "The World's Water." USGS Water Science School. Accessed July 8, 2016. http://water.usgs.gov/edu/earthwherewater.html.

"A Public Outreach Module: Sunlight and Solar Heat: How Are They Made?" Jet Propulsion Laboratory. Accessed July 9, 2016. http://genesismission.jpl.nasa.gov/science/mod3_SunlightSolarHeat/.

"Report Burmese Python Sightings." Florida Fish and Wildlife Conservation Commission. Accessed June 2016. http://myfwc.com/wildlifehabitats/nonnatives/python/report/.

Ruzek, Martin. "Earth System Science in a Nutshell." Starting Point, Science Education Resource Center, Carleton College. Accessed July 9, 2016. http://serc.carleton.edu/introgeo/earthsystem/nutshell/index.html.

"Science Games for Kids: Solids, Liquids, and Gases." Science Kids. Accessed July 20, 2016. http://www.sciencekids.co.nz/gamesactivities/gases.html.

STEM Education in our Florida Schools. PPT. Tallahassee: Florida Department of Education, 2014. Accessed July 2, 2015. www.fldoe.org.

Stille, Darlene. *Energy: Heat, Light, and Fuel (Amazing Science)*. Picture Window Books, 2004.

"Sundial." *Encyclopedia Britannica*. Accessed June 5, 2016. https://www.britannica.com/technology/sundial.

"Thylacine, or Tasmanian Tiger, Thylacinus cynocephalus." Tasmania Parks and Wildlife Service. Accessed June 5, 2016. http://www.parks.tas.gov.au/?base=4765.

"What Is Gravity Really?" NASA Space Place. Accessed July 28, 2016. http://spaceplace.nasa.gov/what-is-gravity/en/.

"What Is Hydroponics?" Controlled Environmental Agricultural Center, University of Arizona. Accessed July 8, 2016. http://ceac.arizona.edu/hydroponics.

Wonders of Water Teacher Guide. The NEED Project. Accessed May 5, 2016. http://www.need.org/files/curriculum/guides/Wonders%20of%20Water%20Teacher.pdf.